ALASTAIR

£14.99/$19.95

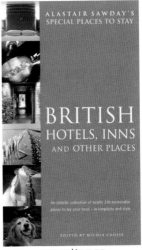

£13.99/$17.95

£14.99/$19.95

£13.99/$19.99

Credit card orders (free p&tp) 01275 464891
www.specialplacestostay.com

In US: credit card orders (800) 243-0495, 9am-5pm EST,
24-hour fax (800) 820-2329 www.globepequot.com

Design:
Caroline King

Maps & Mapping:
Bartholomew Mapping, a division of
HarperCollins, Glasgow

Printing:
Pims, UK

UK Distribution:
Penguin UK, 80 Strand, London

US Distribution:
The Globe Pequot Press, Guilford,
Connecticut

ISBN 1-901970-44-2

Printed in UK on Megamatt: 50% recycled and
de-inked fibres. There is no use of chlorine in
the de-inking process.

ALASTAIR SAWDAY'S
SPECIAL PLACES TO STAY

LONDON

Contents

Guide entries Entry Map

Back Page

We began by chance, in 1993, seeking a job for a friend. On my desk was a file: a miscellany of handsome old houses in France, some that could provide a bed, and some a meal, to strangers.

I ran a small travel company at the time, taking people off the beaten track; these places were our 'finds'. No chain hotels for us, no tourist restaurants if we could possibly visit old manor houses, farms and châteaux whose owners would breathe new life into our enthusiasm for France.

So Jane set off with a file under her arm and began to turn it into a book. We were then innocent enough to ignore advice and print 'far too many' – 10,000. We sold them all, in six months – and a publishing company was born.

We exhorted readers to enjoy a 'warm welcome, wooden beams, stone walls, good coffee' and nailed our colours firmly to the mast: 'We are not impressed by TVs, mini-bars and trouser-presses'. We urged people to enjoy simplicity and authenticity and railed against the iniquities of corporate travel. Little has changed.

Although there are now more than 25 of us working out here in our rural idyll, publishing about 20 books, we are holding tightly to our original ethos and gradually developing it. Our first priority is to publish the best books in our field and to nourish a reputation for integrity. It is critically important that readers trust our judgement.

Our next priority is to sell them – fortunately they sell themselves, too, such is their reputation for reliability and for providing travellers with memorable experiences and friendships.

However, publishing and selling books is not enough. It raises other questions: What is our impact on the world around us? How do we treat ourselves and other people? Is not a company just people working together with a shared focus? So we have begun to consider our responses to those questions and thus have generated our Ethical Policy.

There is little intrinsically ethical about publishing travel guides, but there are ways in which we can improve. Firstly, we use recycled paper and seek the most eco-friendly printing methods. Secondly, we are promoting local economies and encouraging good work. We seek beauty and are providing an alternative to the corporate culture that has done so much damage. Thirdly, we celebrate the use of locally-sourced and organic food

Who are we?

among our owners and have launched a pilot Fine Breakfast scheme in our British B&B guide.

But the way we function as a company matters too. We treat each other with respect and affection. An easy-going but demanding office atmosphere seems to work for us. But for these things to survive we need to engage all the staff, so we are split into three teams: the Green team, the Better Business team and the Charitable Trust team.

Each team meets monthly to advise the company. The Green team uses our annual Environmental Audit as a text and monitors progress. The Better Business team ponders ethical issues such as flexible working, time off in lieu/overtime, and other matters that need a deep airing before decisions are made. The Trust team allocates the small sum that the company gives each year to charities, and raises extra money.

A few examples of our approach to company life: we compost our waste, recycle the recyclable, run a shared car to work, run a car on LPG and as another on a mix of recycled cooking oil and diesel, operate a communal organic food ordering system, use organic or local food for our own events, take part in Bike to Work day, use a 'green' electricity supplier, partially bank with Triodos

(the ethical bank in Bristol), have a health insurance scheme that encourages alternative therapies, and sequester our carbon emissions.

Especially exciting for us is an imminent move to our own eco offices; they will conserve energy and use little of it. But I have left to the end any mention of our most tangible effort in the ethical field: our Fragile Earth series of books. There are The Little Food Book, The Little Earth Book and The Little Money Book – hugely respected and selling solidly – look out for new titles in the Fragile Earth series.

Perhaps the most vital element in our growing Ethical Policy is the sense of engagement that we all have. It is not only stimulating to be trying to do the right thing, but it is an important perspective for us all at work. And that can only help us to continue to produce beautiful books.

Alastair Sawday

Picture
Paul Groom

Acknowledgements

I come to sing the praises of Tom Bell, the architect and inspiration behind this book – and the sole author. He has been adamantine in his determination to do it well – and in his own manner. He has also been unusual in choosing the bicycle as his means of transport; the noble steed has carried him to every place in this book, whatever the weather. For that alone he has my huge respect. I know what it can be like, having turned up to stay in a smart London hotel recently without a square inch of dry skin to my name. (But there is a fringe benefit: the reaction of the hotel staff speaks volumes about the hotel.)

Tom has also been unusual in needing almost no editing; he writes with verve and a sharp ear for modern idiom and style. His deeply held convictions about diversity have found their way into the book in subtle ways. His wide-ranging tastes are manifest in the unusual range of places included, and his fondness for human character and individuality are there in the people he enjoys.

We are proud of this book and are massively grateful to Tom for putting it together, managing its boundless detail and writing it.

Alastair Sawday

Series Editor
Alastair Sawday

Editor
Tom Bell

Editorial Director
Annie Shillito

Managing Editor
Jackie King

Production Manager
Julia Richardson

Web & IT
Russell Wilkinson, Matt Kenefick

Production
Rachel Coe, Paul Groom, Allys Williams

Copy Editor
Jo Boissevain

Editorial
Roanne Finch, Danielle Williams

Sales & Marketing & PR
Siobhan Flynn, Paula Brown, Sarah Bolton

Accounts
Sheila Clifton, Bridget Bishop, Christine Buxton, Jenny Purdy, Sandra Hassell

General London photos
Quentin Craven

Have you ever had to look for somewhere to stay in London? If so, you will be relieved to find the second edition of this guide.

Once upon a time you may have had friends in London with a flat and a floor to sleep upon. But then they moved on and you lost touch. Perhaps some of them now have small children and you can't face another early morning. Or you have such unusual hours that you are loathe to impose yourself on a normal family. Whatever the case – if you have had to book a hotel you may have been astonished by the cost, the awfulness and the aloofness. You may well have been bewildered by the choice and ended up in a tourist hotel in Earl's Court, stuffed with raucous French school children.

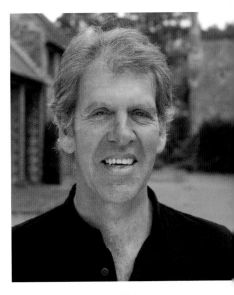

Tom Bell has trawled London for interesting – special – places to stay. 'Special' means that he has avoided the ludicrously over-priced (as opposed to expensive but good value), the ugly, the pompous, the 'naff' and the over-commercial. He also devoted a lot of energy looking for special Bed and Breakfasts. They are wonderful alternatives to hotels, if you need human contact, lower prices and personal flair. And he has found places with a definite 'wow' factor – such as a beautiful little 'visitor' house belonging to a religious community. So the book is a miscellaneous and eclectic guide, just what is needed in a world dominated by the tastes and values of a powerful few.

Alastair Sawday

Picture
Paul Groom

Introduction

A LITTLE SPARKLE, A GOOD CHAT AND DOORS THAT OPEN ONTO MORE HUMAN EXPERIENCES

About this book

This book has a simple aim: to cut out the lottery odds of finding the right place to stay in London.

It is an insider's guide written with outsiders in mind. It has been thoroughly researched, with every property in the book visited – many others did not make the cut. Not for us the life-sapping greys of tedious station B&Bs, nor the identikit interiors of soulless chain hotels. Rather, we go for a little sparkle, a good chat and doors that open onto more human experiences.

What to expect

B&Bs

There are over 80 B&Bs (home stays) in this book. B&Bs are private homes into which owners invite visitors to stay for an agreed price. Some of the homes in this book are grand, others are more modest with correspondingly modest prices.

All are run by owners who live their lives around their guests, and while many will bend over backwards to help – pick you up from the station, get up early to prepare your breakfast, lend you an umbrella or an A-Z – do remember that if you want formal service at the ring of a bell, you will only find it in a hotel.

Hotels

You'll find the odd big name, chic city hideaways, plush country-house-style bolt holes, and trendy designer pads. As a general rule of thumb, the price of a hotel room corresponds to its size, style and centrality; huge, lavishly furnished suites in Mayfair don't come cheap. It is worth remembering that most hotels in London serve the business sector from Monday to Thursday and reduce their prices at weekends to encourage visitors.

Other Places

We wanted this book to appeal to a cross-section of tastes and wallets. In a small crusade to highlight low prices in the city we have included several university halls of residence where guests can stay at reasonable prices during the summer holidays. There are also a couple of hostels with dorm rooms for as little as £10 a night. You will also find a small selection of self-catering properties. These can be stylish and excellent value for money (£500 a week for two), giving total independence. All have good linen, excellent kitchens, shops on the doorstep, and are very easy to 'slip into'. We also include some serviced accommodation: smart, private apartments with full kitchens, and a daily maid service.

Photos

The pictures that we publish are given to us by the owners. It is worth bearing in mind that while hotels employ professional photographers to provide them with a portfolio of seductive images, B&B owners tend to point their Kodak at the bed and hope for the best.

Space

Space is a rare commodity in central London. Thus, to stay in the middle of town will cost a lot more than to stay a couple of miles out. Most Londoners live away from the centre.

Noise

London is a big city with a level of noise that is unavoidable. However, because retail and business districts tend to be quite separate from each other, most residential areas are quiet all day long. Just occasionally you get a bit of noise from a pub at closing time. London is quieter at night than you might expect. If, however, you are a light sleeper, it is always worth asking for a quiet room when you book.

Bedrooms

We list the different types of beds available: singles, twins (two singles), doubles, twin/doubles (twin beds which can be linked to make a double), triples (three singles), family rooms (a double and a single), quadruples (four singles), four-posters and suites (bigger rooms with an open-plan sitting area or a separate sitting room). It is always worth checking exactly what's in your room, how big it is, etc.

Bathrooms

All rooms are 'en suite' unless stated. Some have baths, some have showers, some have both. A *separate* bathroom means you will have the bathroom to yourself, but that you'll need to leave your room to get to it. A *shared* bathroom is also beyond your bedroom door and shared with another guest or the owners. Separate and shared bathrooms are

Introduction

often two paces across the landing and quite lovely. We strongly advise you not to discount properties simply because they do not have 'en suite' bathrooms.

Price

We publish the full rate of a one-night stay for two people sharing a double room; prices for singles, family rooms and suites are given separately. While hotel prices fluctuate wildly, those of B&Bs tend not to. In a B&B, if you decide to stay for a week, your host might agree to a small discount, but this is rare and those who push for a deal may give offence. Things change with hotels. The rates we give – the hotel's rack rates – usually only apply during busy periods. At all other times rates will be lower, often much lower. Ask for the best price; you may be surprised. Exceptions to this rule tend to be hotels with under ten rooms, the big hotels that are famous the world over, and hotels which already have attractive prices. The very best deals are to be found at the very last minute.

All prices include VAT (Value Added Tax). On the phone, hotels usually quote prices without VAT, so check: an extra 17.5% may come as a nasty surprise when you come to pay. If no single occupancy rate is given, it means that single people pay the full whack for a double room. Where you find a price range, this is because some rooms are bigger and smarter than others. Some B&Bs may show a single price for a single bed but charge a small surcharge for single people in a double bed.

Meals

Breakfast is included in the price unless stated. B&Bs usually include breakfast, hotels often don't. Some places offer a full English breakfast of bacon and eggs, sausages and tomatoes; others stick to the continental alternative, but this is usually quite extravagant, with fruits and yogurts, cereals, croissants and toast. B&Bs occasionally offer evening meals, and usually at a communal table, but will need advance warning if you wish to eat in. We have listed local restaurants which hosts have enthusiastically recommended. Where hotels have a restaurant, we have given approximate meal prices. Some offer a small room-service menu, too.

Getting about

The nearest trains, tubes and buses are all given. Although the public transport system comes in for a good deal of criticism, if you travel outside rush hour (7.30am–9.30am, 4pm-7pm) you will always get a seat. Your hosts will know the best ways to get about and will happily advise.

Buses

Ken Livingstone, mayor of London, has expanded the bus system substantially over the last two years, with good results. Buses are not only more frequent and more reliable, they are also a great way to see London. Bus cards cost £2.50 a day, allow unlimited travel and can be bought at most newsagents. Buses are slower than tubes, but the front seat experience on the top deck of a double decker is hard to beat. The letter 'N' before a bus number denotes a night bus and many buses now run 24 hours a day.
The site:
www.transportforlondon.gov.uk/buses
is excellent, interactive and has information on every bus route in town. If you can find one (no easy feat), buy the Greater London Bus Map for £2. If in doubt, London Travel Information (020 7222 1234) will have the answer.

The tube

The tube is the most popular way to get around town, but it can be expensive with a one-way ticket from zone 1 to zone 2 costing a crazy £2.20. Central London travel cards (zones 1 and 2) cost £5.30 a day, £4.30 after 9.30am. They are valid for buses as well. Weekend travel cards (Saturday and Sunday) cost £6.40 (zones 1 and 2). Weekly travel cards (£20.20, zones 1 and 2) are available without a passport

photo. They gives total access to buses and tubes, 24 hours a day. You can get to Heathrow on the Piccadilly line (£3.90) and to City airport via the Docklands Light Railway and the Number 69 bus from Canning Town (£4.70): see www.dlr.co.uk. London Travel Information (020 7222 1234) can answer your questions. Also see www.thetube.com, or the map in this book.

Trains

Local trains into London's big stations are often the quickest way in and out of town. The fast train from Richmond to Waterloo (eight an hour) takes 12 minutes; you can do Crystal Palace to Victoria in 20 minutes. Your hosts will have timetables. Airport trains are useful, too. The Heathrow Express (0845 600 1515) from Paddington Station costs £15 one way, £27 return (five times more than the tube), leaves every 15 minutes (5.10am-23.30), and takes 20 minutes. The Gatwick Express (0845 850 1530) from Victoria Station costs £11 single, £21.50 return, leaves every 15 minutes between 5.50am and midnight (then hourly until 4.30am) and takes about 35 minutes. The Stansted Express (0870 040 9090) from Liverpool Street Station costs £13.80 one way, £24 return, leaves every 30 minutes (on the hour and half past, 5am-11.30pm) and takes 45 minutes. It's quicker than a taxi. As is Eurostar (08705 186 186) which will whisk you off to Paris in three hours (15+ trains a day) or Brussels (ten a day) in two and a half. It leaves from Waterloo Station. Ticket prices start at £59 return and rise in £10 bites up to £189 return. You can book 90 days in advance, but you don't have to book too far ahead to get a good deal (see www.eurostar.com). National Rail Enquiries (08457 484950) will tell you the time of any train in Britain. Also see www.thretrainline.com.

Driving and the Congestion Charge

If you want to drive in central London, you'll have to pay to do so. The current charge is £5 a day, though if you don't pay by 10pm,

the cost rises to £10, or £40 if you forget. Call 0845 90 1234 or see www.cclondon.com.

Parking

If you do bring you car, don't expect the congestion charge to be the only cost you incur. The cost of parking depends on where you want to park. In central London you should expect to pay about £35 a day, maybe more. As you move away from the centre, the price drops bit by bit: Kensington, Chelsea and Notting Hill will cost about £20 a day; Fulham, Camden and Islington about £15; Kennington, Hammersmith and Brook Green about £10, then out to Streatham, Tooting, Chiswick, Crouch Hill and the price tumbles to about £5. You will save considerable amounts of money, time and bother by leaving your car at home and using public transport.

Walking

In central London walking is the best way to get around. You can cut through parks and back streets and step off the tourist trail. The best thing you can do is buy an A-Z, the London street guide; it's available just about anywhere. They cost £5 you won't get lost if you have one. Various walking tours exist and are usually priced at about £5. Try Original London Walks (020 7624 3978 or www.walks.com). London Open House (020 7267 7644) run tours every Saturday. They are more expensive (£18.50), but worth it. They walk you round London's great buildings, both old and new, and spill the historical beans as they do. The same people also organise the Open House Weekend in the third week of September, which sees the doors of London's finest buildings thrown open to anyone who wants to take a look. It's free and gets Londoners out in their thousands.

Cycling

The quickest way to get around town, but London's streets are packed and you should expect no niceties from drivers. You can rent mountain bikes or hybrids from the London Bicycle Tour Company (020 7928 6838) at 1a Gabriel's Wharf, 56 Upper Ground, SE1: £12 first day, £6 second, £36 a week, credit card deposit required; they also lead bike tours and you can hire roller blades, too. If the idea of cycling around London is too scary, head to Richmond Park and a very pretty eight-mile cycling perimeter track. In summer, you can hire bikes by the hour at Roehampton Gate, with four hours costing £12 (07050 209 249). It's a fantastic day out, very popular, and Richmond Park is easily London's most beautiful. There are food and drink stalls along the route or you can bring a picnic.

Taxis

Taxis are quite expensive and their prices rise still further after 10pm, though you should try a black cab once. Drivers are all licensed and you can hail them on the street. Mini cabs – ordinary cars – are less expensive, but not as stylish, and you have to ring for them. Never pick one up on the streets, where taxi touts – unregistered drivers – operate. Addison Lee is a reliable firm and covers the whole of London (020 7387 8888). Lady Cabs (020 7272 3300) has mostly female drivers. Always ask the price when you're on the phone.

Boats

Boats from Westminster Pier to Greenwich run all year round and cost £6.50 one way, £8.20 return

Practical matters
Deposits

You should expect to book your accommodation in advance, and to pay a deposit. If you cancel your booking expect to lose the deposit – or at least, some of it – unless your room is re-let, in which case you may have it refunded in full. Check the exact terms when booking and have the B&B or hotel confirm the agreement in writing.

Credit cards

In hotels, Visa and MasterCard are universally accepted, American Express is sometimes, Diners Card hardly ever. B&Bs rarely accept credit cards and expect payment in cash or by British cheque.

(you get a one-third reduction with a travel card). The trip takes about an hour. Westminster to Hampton Court (via Richmond and Kew Gardens) runs from April to October and costs £12 one way or £18 return. The trip takes about three hours one way, so travel there or back by train (Hampton Court station). Trains go to/from Waterloo, via Clapham Junction or Vauxhall and take 30 minutes.

Telephones

The per-unit cost of telephoning from hotels is usually exorbitant (probably £1 a minute, local). Check the per-minute cost before making a call. Hotels often give vague answers to this question, but manage to be extremely precise on your bill. The code for America from England is 011.

Both trips are well worth the time and money. Most other boats operating on the Thames leave from Westminster Pier, The Embankment, SW1 (Westminster tube). London Travel Information (020 7222 1234) has timetables; or, see www.transportforlondon.gov.uk/river.

The internet

Most hotels have internet connection. Some have a single computer you can use, some have modems in all bedrooms, some have hi-speed services, some even wifi systems (wireless connectivity) that allow you to use the TV in

Introduction

most hotels aren't. B&B owners will often give you an ashtray (and an umbrella) and let you explore their garden. Most hotels have only a few rooms put aside for smokers, many do not allow smoking in bedrooms at all. If you want a smoke-free room, you are certain to get it.

Children

Child-friendly B&Bs may not have all the kit that a child-friendly hotel would have. Please don't assume there will be cots etc. In the hotels, baby-listening and baby-sitting services are often available. Do check your requirements with owners and managers when booking.

Problems, problems

If you have a problem, however trivial you may think it is, always feel justified to bring it to the attention of your host, the owner or manager; they are primed, one hopes, to solve it at a stroke. Owners always say 'if only I'd known' when we contact them retrospectively. Do give them that chance. If, however, you do and get nowhere, please let us know.

Booking agencies

Some of the B&Bs listed in this book use agencies to take their bookings. If the B&B you want to stay in is not available, the agencies may suggest another property that does not appear in this book and that we have not seen.

your bedroom to access the net. Sometimes they charge, sometimes they don't. If you want the full hi-tech works, check when you book. B&Bs tend not to put computers in your room, but owners will often let you pick up e-mails on their personal computers.

Laundry

The majority of places will do laundry for you, or let you do it yourself. Hotels do this as a matter of course, but if you ask a B&B owner, they will nearly always oblige (especially if you are staying for three or four nights). A small fee will usually be charged.

Smoking

A symbol tells you if a place is totally non-smoking. Most B&Bs are;

Subscriptions
All the places chosen for this book have paid a small fee to be included in it. This helps with the high production costs that come with an all-colour book. But this is a fee, not a bribe. People cannot buy their way in.

And a final word on congestion charging...

The introduction of congestion charging in 2003 has been hailed by many – retailers excepted – as an immense success. The number of cars and lorries entering the central zone has dropped by 16%, with congestion slashed by 30%, accidents down by 20% and journey times reduced by 14%. It has generated piles of cash – £68 million in the first year – with the potential to yield over £100 million a year once improved enforcement procedures are put in place. Some noticeable reinvestment of profits into the capital's transport network is to be lauded, and London's recently replenished armada of buses now move with ever-greater ease despite an extra 15,000 Londoners on board daily. However, there is also cause for concern. Mayor Ken Livingstone recently hinted that the congestion charge may have to rise because not enough of us are driving into town. Revenues are lower than forecast and next year's profits have already been allocated. So much for the scheme that he assured us

was set up to cut congestion, not to raise money.

As for London's streets, they remain clogged with traffic, which is, of course, the point. Congestion charging is not a solution to traffic, it is a way of making money out of it, and its seemingly successful introduction into London means one thing: you are going to pay more often when you drive. The central London congestion zone is likely to be enlarged, there is talk of a toll on the M4 to Heathrow, perhaps even one for the whole of the M25. That's just the start of it. Around the country and around the world, local and national governments are rubbing their hands at the prospect of practicing licensed alchemy. What appears to be a radical solution to

an urban problem is slowly revealing itself as an old establishment trick: hijack the moral high ground, then cash in on it.

The way to reduce traffic in cities is very simple: ban it wherever possible. Rome's yearly car-free weekend has become something of a carnival, with families taking picnics onto the streets and reclaiming their city from the oppression of the automobile. When introduced permanently, car-free areas rejuvenate cities, bring locals and tourists out by the hatful, make streets safer and more pleasant, encourage people to shop locally, create closer neighbourhood ties, cut crime and reduce harmful emissions. Traffic could be slashed by over 60%. School buses for children can ferry kids to class, lorries can come to deliver, bicycles, scooters and motorbikes can zip about the place, taxis and buses can carry us to the tube and railway stations. What we need to do is stop using cars. The notion that we must keep driving in order to pay for a greener future and a better public transport system is risible.

consumer, you check out the alternatives – train, bus and aeroplane – and you discover that canny local government officials have undercut the competition in order to secure income. Might it be that in the long run congestion charging will not cut traffic at all, but do the opposite? Time will tell, but in the meantime we heartily recommend that you leave your car at home.

Tom Bell

As for the future, well, imagine a world, say 20 years hence, when driving has become a commodity and every mile you cover is charged. Does this stop you using your car? Quite the reverse. Like any good

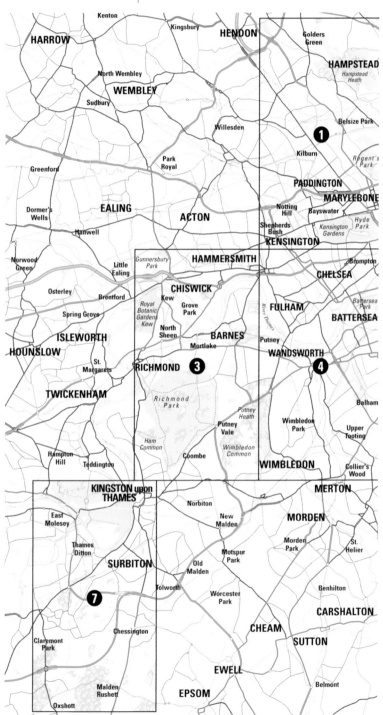

©Bartholomew Ltd, 2004

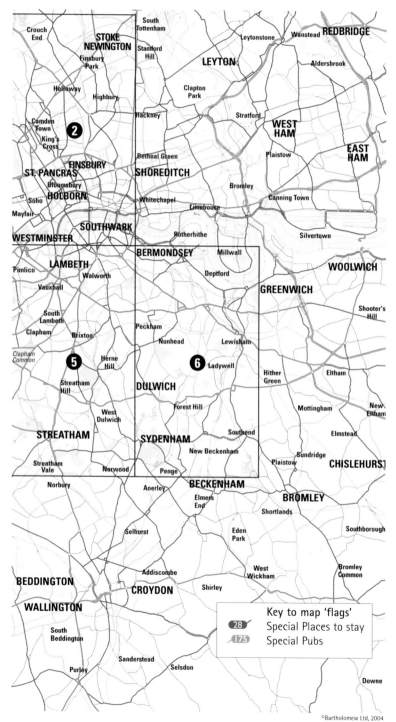

Key to map 'flags'
- **28** Special Places to stay
- **175** Special Pubs

©Bartholomew Ltd, 2004

1: 50,000

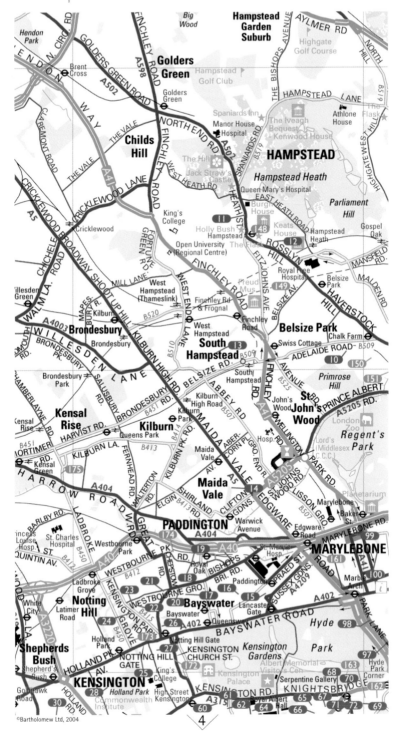

Map 2

27

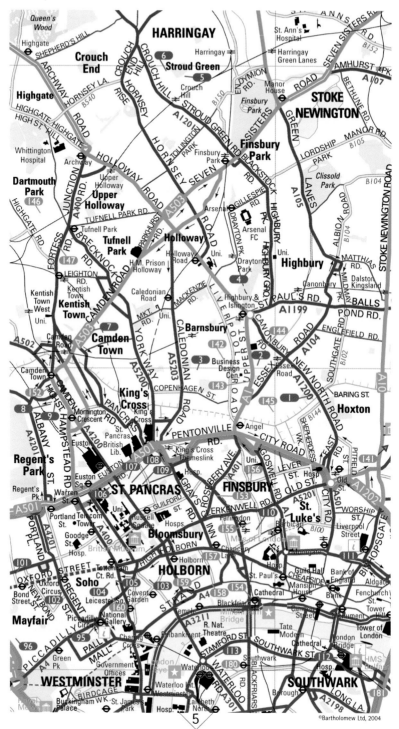

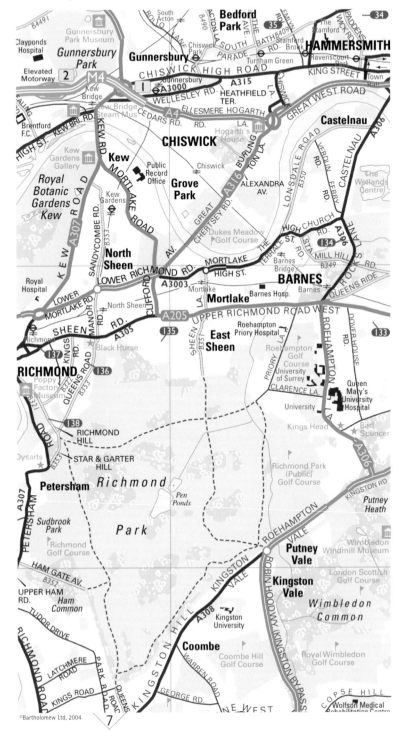

Map 4

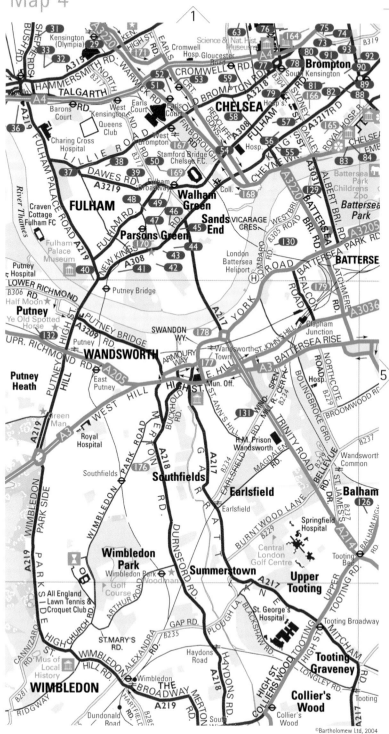

©Bartholomew Ltd, 2004

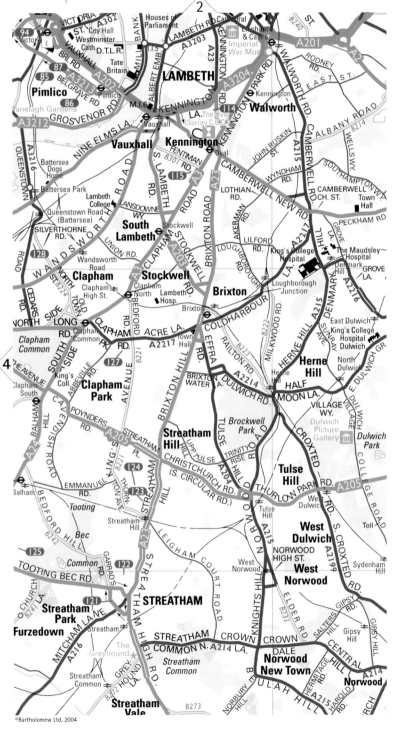

Map 6

31

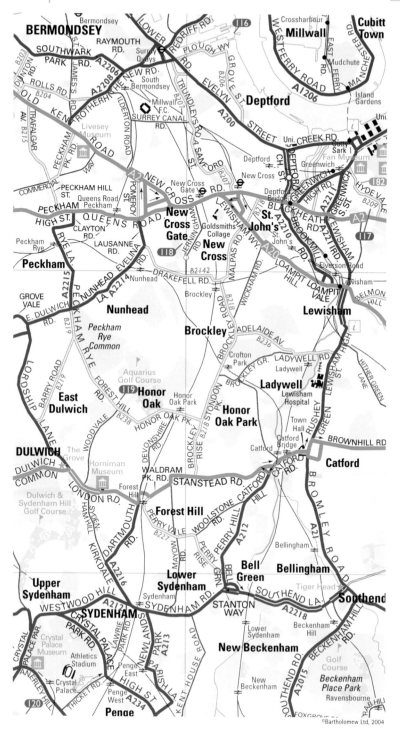

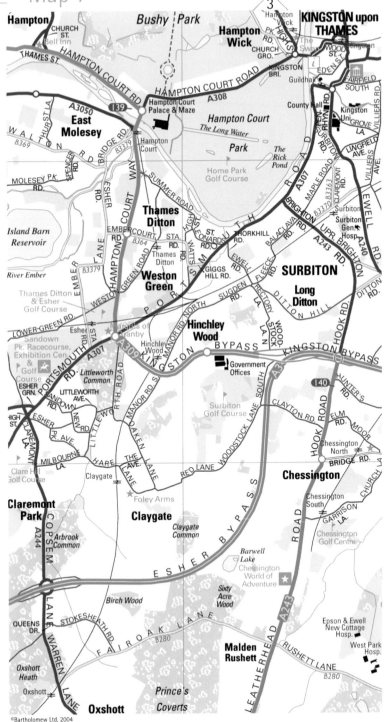

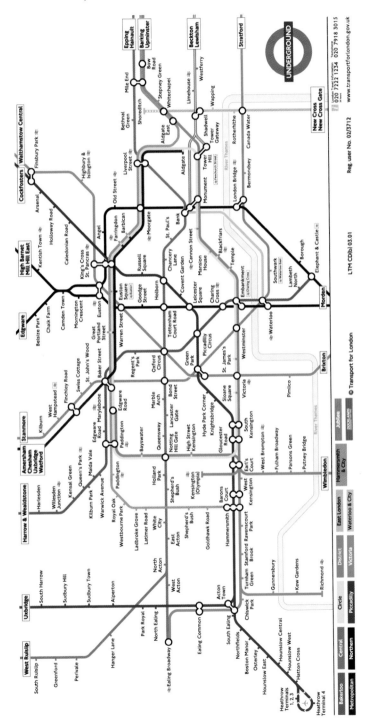

north

- **Hampstead Heath:** London's northernmost park, with great views from Parliament Hill Fields
- **Hampstead village:** a haunt for the literary and the famous
- **Primrose Hill:** more views, slightly more 'alternative' living
- **Regent's Park:** boating lake, open-air theatre and London Zoo
- **Kenwood House, on the edge of the Heath:** 18th-century house, lake and gardens, summer concerts
- **Keat's House in South End Green**
- **Highgate Cemetery**
- **Lord's Cricket ground and museum**
- **Camden:** young, lively, cosmopolitan area with London's biggest market; take the canal boat from Little Venice
- **Islington:** residential enclave for media types and politicians, with eclectic restaurants and shops

Arlington Avenue
Islington, London N1

Richard's fabulous 1848 townhouse is a real find — incredible value for money a short walk from Islington (you can follow the Grand Union Canal up). Inside you find a world of books and art (Richard is a writer and teacher). A bust looks skywards in the marble fireplace, the windows are dressed in elegant shutters, exhilarating art hangs on the walls. There is a hint of bohemia to the place, though the influences are mostly classical, viz. the old radiators, the winged armchair and the small chandelier. Arlington Avenue is closed to through traffic, thus remarkably quiet. The bedroom, at the top of the house, overlooks several gardens to the back; it's simply furnished — bed, chair, wardrobe, lilac walls — but strikingly so. The shiny white bathroom is shared and two flights down, but if you don't mind that, you've struck gold. Shop locally, eat picnic suppers in the red and gold dining room, chill drinks in the fridge. You make your own breakfast; Richard will do your shopping or you can bring your own, then prepare it whenever you want (late risers welcome). This is laissez-faire B&B and it's fantastic.

rooms	1 double sharing bath & shower.
price	£35-£40. Singles £30.
meals	Self-catering (breakfast only); full kitchen facilities available.
closed	Occasionally.
tube	Old Street; Angel (both a 10-minute walk).
bus	19, 38, 56, 73, 76, 141, 271.

	Richard Hayman
tel	07711 265 183
e-mail	arlington.avenue@virgin.net

B&B

Map 2 Entry 1

26 Florence Street
Islington, London N1 2FW

I am under strict orders to mention the theatres around here, especially the Almeida, its reputation so strong that Juliette Binoche, Kevin Spacey and Cate Blanchette have all been drawn to tread its boards. Valerie comes from a theatrical background, a fact apparent after a milli-second in her vibrant home: sparkling cushions, flourishing colour, incense and wall-hangings – the house is packed with pieces from Morocco, Italy, India and beyond. The bedroom is equally stylish with old Irish linen, stencilled window seats, rugs galore and a sofa covered in throws. There's a private Shaker-style bathroom and a tropical conservatory, which guests can use – Eden in N1. Breakfast is upstairs in the Aga-warmed kitchen/dining room. Here, amid more rustic chic, you breakfast on brioche, croissants from Euphorium, juice and yogurt, fruit and coffee. There's an organic farmers market on Sundays, masses of shops, antiques on Camden Passage (Wednesdays and Saturdays) and hundreds of brilliant restaurants to tempt you. Try Carluccio's, the Italian deli; the locals queue down the street for it.

rooms	1 double with separate shower.
price	£90–£95. Singles from £70.
meals	Continental breakfast included.
closed	Occasionally.
tube	Angel; Highbury and Islington.
bus	4, 19, 38, 73.

	Valerie Rossmore
tel	020 7359 5293
e-mail	valerie.rossmore@virgin.net

B&B

Map 2 Entry 2

52 Hemingford Road
Islington, London N1 1DB

These artisans' houses were built in 1830 by Lord Thornhill. He had seven daughters, who gave their collective name to nearby Seven Sisters. Deirdre, trained nurse and freelance aromatherapist, gives a mean Indian head massage, so come for the healing properties of her easy-going home. You get big mirrors, the odd wall hanging, throws on the sofas and scented candles. It's a light and airy place, simple and homely, with dashes of colour and comforting style. There's furniture which Deirdre's grandmother inherited, then passed down to her, the stripped pine doors are original, there are window boxes and watercolours. Upstairs, the double at the back is in country style, with scatter cushions on a big old bed, a pretty dresser and garden views. Downstairs, the larger room is whimsically furnished (viz. the shoe cupboard from a South Kensington prep school) and comes with a sofa, an armchair, a TV, CD and DVD players and a compact shower room. Breakfast is a help-yourself affair, you can order pizza at night and eat in the kitchen or decamp to the garden for summer picnics.

rooms	3: 1 twin; 1 double, 1 occasional single sharing bath & shower (same-party bookings only).
price	£55-£60. Singles £45.
meals	Continental breakfast included.
closed	Occasionally.
train	Caledonian Road (North London Line)
tube	Angel (10-minute walk).
bus	17, 91, 153, 259, 274.

	Deirdre Walker
tel	020 7609 3335
e-mail	deirdwalker@aol.com

B&B

Map 2 Entry 3

4 Highbury Terrace
Highbury, London N5 1UP

To quote from a letter Marion wrote after we'd met: "Thanks for your visit, sorry we talked so much… the books you left herewith returned… I will get to bed now; a need to meet a breakfast at 4.30am has arisen." Marion and Donn transcend the art of convivial hospitality; nothing is too much trouble, everything is a natural response, and they will think these words of praise just so much pretty hogwash. A house of laughter, of wandering conversations and spontaneous diversions, where books are brought out to check facts while the kettle works overtime. Nothing is done to impress, which is why everything does. Their 1779 home overlooks the peace and quiet of Highbury Fields (a short walk across it takes you to the tube). Inside, the simple décor is warm and homely, and light floods in through myriad Georgian windows, one 14 feet high. Comfy bedrooms, fresh flowers, pretty linen, throws over chairs, the odd piece from Ikea – nothing jars. The top floor has two bedrooms, kitchen, shower and bath, thus perfect for families. Islington's bars and cafés are on your doorstep. A great find.

rooms	3: 2 twins, both with separate bath; 1 single, separate shower & wc.
price	£60-£70. Singles from £35.
meals	Continental breakfast included.
closed	Occasionally.
train	Highbury & Islington.
tube	Highbury & Islington; Holloway Road.
bus	4, 19, 30, 43.

	Marion & Donn Barnes
tel	020 7354 3210

B&B

Map 2 Entry 4

20 Ossian Road

Crouch End, London N4 4EA

Ann and John have travelled the world; they are both from Cork and tell a good story. Their home is quietly stylish – smart without being manicured, pretty without being twee. It's nicely over-the-top in parts. "I like a bit of glamour," says Ann, and that's pretty much what you get: French antique beds, a virtual four-poster, a flurry of cushions, a big armoire. Fresh flowers tumble out of urns on top of wardrobes, muslin drapes fall from the ceiling to crown the bed. There are small chandeliers and splashes of colour. You get Laura Ashley bedding, Egyptian cotton, piles of pillows and fluffy bathrobes. Breakfast downstairs in the dining room (throws on the sofa, loads of cushions, a big gilt mirror) is hearty and often quite social. The fire gets lit in winter, so you can roast away while you scoff your bacon and eggs. You get the full English, kippers if you want them, or a proper vegetarian alternative. Ann will pick you up from the station, there's internet access at the house. A very informal, friendly little place, and old travellers who miss the open road will love it; the comforts are real, but the spirit lives on.

rooms	3: 2 twins/doubles, 1 double.
price	£65. Singles £45.
meals	Full English breakfast included.
closed	Occasionally.
train	Harringay (to King's Cross).
tube	Finsbury Park (10-minute walk).
bus	W3, 91.

	Ann & John O'Connor
tel	020 8340 4331
fax	020 8340 8331
e-mail	ann@ossianguesthouse.co.uk
web	www.ossianguesthouse.co.uk

B&B

Map 2 Entry 5

31 Mountview Road

Crouch End, London N4 4SS

Odette is perfect for B&B – a kind, gentle smiler who loves having people in her home. Her house – a top-to-toe renovation – is delightful: crisply uncluttered, airy and elegant. In the hallway the original 1882 stained-glass windows survive, as does the parquet flooring. There are yellow walls, high ceilings and big windows that flood the place with light. The big open-plan kitchen/dining room is warmly chic, yet homely, too, and you can chat to Odette as she cooks your breakfast. Doors open onto a small but lush garden that you're welcome to use. Bedrooms upstairs are dreamy. The big double at the front is exceptional, with a huge Flemish wardrobe, ragged ochre on the walls, rugs on the floor and a view over London. Odette does all the upholstery herself – the plush armchairs, the waffled bed covers, the pretty curtains: exceptional stuff. The rooms at the back are smaller (and less expensive), but equally pretty. Expect stripped wooded floors, cane furniture, good linen, and a smart rustic feel. Alexander Palace (and Park) is close by and Odette will pick you up from the station when you arrive.

rooms	4: 1 twin, 1 double; 1 double, 1 single sharing bath & shower.
price	£50–£70. Singles £40.
meals	Full English breakfast included.
closed	Occasionally.
train	Harringay (to King's Cross).
tube	Finsbury Park (15-minute walk).
bus	W3, W7, 91.

	Odette & Daniel Hendrickx
tel	020 8340 9222
fax	020 8342 8494
e-mail	mountviewbb@aol.com
web	www.mountviewguesthouse.com

B&B

Map 2 Entry 6

66 Camden Square
Camden Town, London NW1 9XD

A Japanese-style house in a London square, made of glass and African teak. Rodger designed and built his home as an experiment in the minimal use of materials. It is a real treat: cool, yet comfortable, contemporary, yet lived-in, with all the little touches you'd expect from a professional: halogen lighting, porthole mirrors in the bathroom and a pyramid of glass on the roof that brightens still further. Rodger and Sue have travelled widely, and much from abroad decorates their home. The minimalist feel throughout is in keeping with the Japanese spirit. African teak (iroko) is everywhere, including the stairs which you climb to your bedrooms. These are in Japanese style: paper lanterns, low-slung beds, modern chairs, no clutter. Both rooms have contemporary, blue-and-red stained glass windows, and the double has two walls of glass. You breakfast downstairs at a big wooden table looking onto a courtyard garden full of life. There's Peckham the parrot, too. Trendy Camden has several markets (Camden Lock is great for clothes), Regent's Park, canal walks, the Jazz Café and the Round House Theatre.

rooms	2: 1 double, 1 single sharing bath (same-party bookings only).
price	£90. Singles £45–£55.
meals	Continental breakfast included.
closed	Occasionally.
tube	Camden Town.
bus	24, 27, 29, 31, 88, 168, 274.

	Sue & Rodger Davis
tel	020 7485 4622
fax	020 7485 4622
e-mail	rodgerdavis@btopenworld.com

B&B

Map 2 Entry 7

78 Albert Street
Camden Town, London NW1 7NR

The brains behind this operation belong to Joanna, a psychotherapist; she does all the hard work, leaving Peter to bask in the limelight. He's an exceptional photographer, has snapped his way around the world ("I've been everywhere; I'm very old"), and his pictures (Cape Horn to Kathmandu) hang on the walls, causing traffic jams on the staircase. He's an architect, too, and this house is immaculate from top to toe. The upstairs kitchen is a room of huge style. Look carefully and you'll see how he's lined up the floor tiles with the kitchen units so the lines flow. What you can't see are the floor-to-ceiling windows, the lime-green day bed, the wall of books and the library steps. Head skywards and you find an attractive bunk room for kids (or adults; they're big enough) with a small library of children's books, then a delightful lilac double with windows looking onto a leafy street. In between, you come across an electric-green bathroom with bath foam in a carafe. There are loads of great restaurants close by; try Mignon's for the best Lebanese.

rooms	2: 1 twin/double, 1 room with bunkbeds, sharing bath.
price	£90–£110. Singles £45.
meals	Continental breakfast included.
closed	Occasionally.
tube	Camden Town.
bus	24, 27, 29, 31, 88, 168, 274.

	Joanna & Peter Bell
tel	020 7387 6813
e-mail	joanna@peterbellarchitects.co.uk

B&B

Map 2 Entry 8

Albert Street
Camden Town, London NW1

Great value for money in the poshest street in Camden, only a three-minuite walk from the tube. Elspeth once taught textiles at the Chelsea School of Art, but these days she works for herself, making pillow cases, T-shirts, shoulder bags; you may be tempted. Don't come looking for designer B&B; do come if you want a great welcome, a good chat and pretty bedrooms. The double is a couple of floors up, looks onto the street and comes with a bed made by Elspeth's father (creativity runs in the blood). There are a couple of ancient oak chairs, cheerful linen and loads of books (Granta). Lots of original art, too, most of which comes from within the family and is rather good. The next-door single is a bit of a coup, a lovely room generously priced. You get a shiny wooden bed, great art, terracotta-coloured walls and loads of magazines. Breakfast on brioches, croissants, muffins and fruit in the smart dining room at the front of the house, with views through the big window onto the street. Regent's Park, Camden Lock and Primrose Hill are all close by, and there's Shakespeare in the park in summer.

rooms	2: 1 double, 1 single sharing bath.
price	£65. Singles £35.
meals	Continental breakfast included.
closed	Occasionally.
tube	Camden Town.
bus	24, 27, 29, 31, 88, 168, 274.

The London Bed & Breakfast Agency
tel   020 7586 2768
fax   020 7586 6567
e-mail   stay@londonbb.com

B&B

Map 2 Entry 9

30 King Henry's Road
Primrose Hill, London NW3 3RP

When it comes to writing the definitive book on London B&Bs, Carole will get a chapter of her own. And rightly so; no one has done more to get great London B&Bs up and running, encouraging just about everyone she knows with a good house to start (including at least 10 in this book). So come and stay and see how it's done. Stripped wooden floors in the grandish entrance hall; big rooms, bright and airy, with high ceilings and a smart family feel. Pots and pans hang in the kitchen, the Aga warms the room. Seagrass runs through the house, and there are walls of books on the landing. In the bedroom expect country-house style with a brass bed, bathrobes, crisp linen and old mahogany furniture. The steel and marble kitchen, with open fire in winter, is the place for breakfast: bagels, rolls, croissants, toast, juice, fruit salad and yogurt. Walk in Primrose Hill; Regent's Park is close by, too. You can stroll down Chalk Farm Road to Camden Lock Market, and the restaurants round here are excellent: Odette's is a favourite and Limonia is a Greek place with a big reputation.

rooms	1 twin/double.
price	£100. Singles £80.
meals	Continental breakfast included.
closed	Occasionally.
tube	Chalk Farm.
bus	24, 31, 168.

	Carole Cox
tel	020 7483 2871
fax	020 7483 2871
e-mail	mail@carolecox.co.uk

B&B

Map 1 Entry 10

La Gaffe
107-111 Heath Street, Hampstead, London NW3 6SS

You get real Italian hospitality at La Gaffe. Bernardo and Androulla Stella opened the restaurant in 1962, adding the rooms in 1976. Today it's run with the same easy charm by their sons, Lorenzo and Salvatore. Locals pop in for a chat or a coffee and Lorenzo keeps an eye out for the traffic wardens. Expect delicious traditional Italian cooking – maybe grilled sardines in garlic and olive oil or veal escalope in a lemon sauce; oils, cheeses and hams come from an uncle's farm in Abruzzo. There are muralled walls in the restaurant, where Clint Eastwood was a regular in the Sixties. The hotel stands on the site of five former shepherd's cottages. Bedrooms aren't huge, but have pretty floral fabrics. Those at the back look onto a quiet Georgian square and two have steam baths. You're across the road from Hampstead Heath: walk through the woods, past the ponds and up to Parliament Hill for the best views over London. The village itself is full of terraced cafés, smart boutiques and charming back streets (including Church Row, said to be the most beautiful in London). A family-run gem. Don't miss the meatballs.

rooms	18: 6 doubles, 4 twins, 4 singles, 3 four-posters, 1 family.
price	£95-£125. Singles from £70.
meals	Continental breakfast included. Lunch & dinner, £5-£25.
closed	Occasionally.
tube	Hampstead.
bus	46, 268.

	Lorenzo Stella
tel	020 7435 8965
fax	020 7794 7592
e-mail	la-gaffe@msn.com
web	www.lagaffe.co.uk

Restaurant with Rooms

Map 1 Entry 11

Hampstead Village Guesthouse

2 Kemplay Road, Hampstead, London NW3 1SY

There's nothing mild about the eccentricity here: beds come out of wardrobes, there are tiny, Heath Robinson, Victorian brass-piped showers, and toasters appear from bushes in the garden on fine days. One room has a hidden basin salvaged from a train, another a four-poster bed that once belonged to a German countess, and which moves on rails so she could lie in the sun without getting out of bed. Annemarie is clearly an Olympic champion when it comes to rummaging around in junk/antique shops. Every room has something 'different,' be it a piano, a collection of old LPs and a record player, or a bath in the middle of the room. Coffee comes in mugs with a map of the tube, so you can plan your day while you have breakfast. There are phones in the rooms, and you can also rent mobiles while you stay and pay as you go. It's a three-minute walk to Hampstead Heath – make sure you get to Parliament Hill. Keats-House is round the corner; the poet composed *Ode to a Nightingale* in its garden. You can stop for a drink at the Freemasons Arms, or head to Zen or La Giraffe for great food.

rooms	9: mix of twins, doubles, singles and family rooms; 6 are en suite, 3 share one shower.
price	£72–£120. Singles £48–£90.
meals	Breakfast, optional, £7.
closed	Never.
train	Hampstead Heath (North London Line).
tube	Hampstead.
bus	24, 46, 168, 268.

	Annemarie Van Der Meer
tel	020 7435 8679
fax	020 7794 0254
e-mail	info@hampsteadguesthouse.com
web	www.hampsteadguesthouse.com

B&B

Map 1 Entry 12

79 Greencroft Gardens
South Hampstead, London NW6 3LJ

This is quite some house – big and grand, yet unmistakably a family home. You enter an impressively large hall where the original black and white tiles survive. In the garden a japonica was flowering in February. Penelope makes quince jelly from it (you can try it at breakfast). She also magics quince cheese out of it, so the double Gloucester was brought out and we had a tasting. A place for cricket lovers: Lord's is a 20-minute stroll. Back at the house expect some style. The highlight is the dining room. You'll find rugs, old oils, gilt mirrors, a collection of glove stretchers (only in England…), a grandfather clock and a grand piano on which an aspidistra flourishes. It gives the room a distinctly 20s feel; you expect to be joined by Hercule Poirot for breakfast. Elsewhere, double doors open onto a pretty garden – you can eat out in summer – and exceptional art hangs on the wall. Bedrooms are country-house in style (loads of books, original fireplaces, old wooden furniture, pretty linen); the double is huge. Penelope is great fun, well-travelled and interesting. There are bundles of good restaurants locally, too.

rooms	2: 1 double; 1 single with separate bath.
price	£100. Singles £50.
meals	Full English breakfast included.
closed	Occasionally.
tube	Finchley Road; Swiss Cottage.
bus	13, 82.

Penelope Stanford
tel	020 7624 7849
fax	020 7624 7849
e-mail	penny@lyndonstanford.freeserve.co.uk

B&B

Map 1 Entry 13

west

- **Science Museum, Victoria & Albert Museum, Natural History Museum:** the Cromwell Rd/Exhibition Rd axis finds London's 'big three'
- **Royal Albert Hall:** world-renowned summer Proms
- **Kensington Gardens:** Serpentine Gallery, Princess Diana Memorial Garden, Peter Pan statue, Albert Memorial, lake
- **Holland Park:** open-air theatre, peacocks and squirrels
- **High Street Kensington, King's Road and Fulham Road:** stylish mix of white stucco houses, high street stores, antique shops, boutiques, restaurants and bars
- **Notting Hill:** boho-chic shopping streets, eateries and bars, with multi-cultural Portobello Market and Notting Hill Carnival (August)
- **Fulham:** London's first boom in gentrification

Europa House
79A Randolph Avenue, Maida Vale, London W9 1DW

This is Little Venice, one of London's prettiest quarters, where the Grand Union Canal sweeps gracefully past leafy avenues. Lord's is on your doorstep, as is Regent's Park, but you may wish to spurn them both for the communal gardens that hide behind the smart houses of Randolph Avenue. Expect three and a half acres of weeping willows, well-kept lawns and absolute peace. These serviced apartments are equally divine – big and airy, extremely comfortable, nicely private – each one a suite of rooms with a separate sitting room, a fully-equipped kitchen and a sparkling marble bathroom. The style is warm and uncluttered – glass tables, big sofas, spacious halls, trim carpets – with an open-plan feel throughout. Beds are dressed in crisp linen and warmed by mohair blankets, and apartments at the back have garden views. There are hi-fis, videos, video entrance phones; some rooms have air-conditioners and bamboo floors. You can cook for yourself (there's a supermarket close by), but local restaurants will tempt you out. Don't miss Raoul's for great eggs Benedict, or Jason's for fabulous fish. Brilliant.

rooms	13 apartments: 1 1-bedroom, 8 2-bedroom, 1 3-bedroom, 1 4-bedroom.
price	1-bedroom £175; 2-bedroom £260-£285; 3-bedroom £425; 4-bedroom £500.
meals	Self-catering; full kitchen facilities.
closed	Never.
train	Paddington (to Heathrow).
tube	Warwick Avenue; Maida Vale.
bus	6, 16, 46, 98.

	Linda Campbell
tel	020 7724 5924
fax	020 7724 2937
e-mail	linda@westminsterapartments.co.uk
web	www.westminsterapartments.co.uk

Serviced accommodation

Map 1 Entry 14

The Royal Park Hotel

3 Westbourne Terrace, Lancaster Gate, London W2 3UL

A three-minute stroll will take you into Hyde Park, where you can sit amid the splendour of the Italian Water Gardens and watch the birds bathe. As for Westbourne Terrace, it was once described as 'the finest street in London' (Aldous Huxley lived for a time at No 155), and the houses here are on a grand scale; you can easily imagine the carriages trundling up to the door in Victorian times. The Royal Park is a top-to-toe renovation, three Grade II-listed houses rolled into one, all now stuffed with pretty things. The décor is striking – grand yet uncluttered, with stripped wood floors, Georgian greens and reds on the walls, and sofas clad in the plushest hand-embroidered fabrics. Arrive at tea-time and you will be served scones and jams in one of the two small drawing rooms; come at seven for champagne and canapés on the house. Bedrooms are impeccable, generous with their beds, mattresses, pillows and bathrooms. There are antique desks, flat-screen TVs, and breakfast is brought to your room on a butler's tray, with white linen cloths in silver napkin rings. *Weekend rates from £145 for two, breakfast included.*

rooms	48: 2 singles, 33 twins/doubles, 2 four-posters, 11 suites.
price	£210-£225. Four-posters £260. Suites £300-£345. Singles £180.
meals	Continental breakfast £9.95. 24-hour room service.
closed	Never.
train	Paddington (to Heathrow)
tube	Paddington; Lancaster Gate.
bus	12, 94.

	Daniela Meyer
tel	020 7479 6600
fax	020 7479 6601
e-mail	info@theroyalpark.com
web	www.theroyalpark.com

Hotel

Map 1 Entry 15

Atlantic Paddington

1 Queens Gardens, Paddington, London W2 3BA

An incredible 125,000 people pass through these doors each year, making this one of London's most slept-in buildings. They come for the combination of low prices and central location that make this hostel a must for those in town on a budget. Dorm rooms come for as little as £12 (this price rises in summer), though you never share with more than five others. Basic rooms are 'male' or 'female', but come with a group of friends and you get a room to yourselves. Some are quite big with high ceilings, others are smaller, all have bunk beds, duvets, wardrobes and TVs. Don't expect frills; do expect a friendly welcome and helpful staff. A third of the rooms have their own showers (and cost a little more); a couple have French windows onto small balconies. A continental breakfast is served in the ground-floor dining room, but if you want the full cooked works, try the local greasy spoon. The basement bar is open until 2am and comes with table football, pool and a juke box. There are free daily papers, internet access and secure luggage storage, too.

rooms	212: A mix of singles, twins, triples, quads, five-bed and six-bed rooms. Some twins have their own showers; others share showers.
price	Dorms from £12 p.p.; twins from £20 p.p. Singles from £20 p.p.
meals	Continental breakfast included.
closed	Never.
train	Paddington (to Heathrow).
tube	Paddington; Bayswater.
bus	7, 12, 23, 27, 36, 94.

	Tony Fisher
tel	020 7262 4471
fax	020 7706 8548
e-mail	reservations@atlantic-paddington.com
web	www.atlantic-paddington.com

Hostel

Map 1 Entry 16

The Westminster Hotel
16 Leinster Square, Westbourne Grove, London W2 4PR

The Westminster is a neat little discovery – warm and cosy, nice and central, very well-priced – and although its rooms are mostly generic, it has an unexpected style that belies the fact that this is a biggish tourist hotel. It is also in the throes of a quiet makeover, with florals on the way out and a warm minimalism on the way in. Outside, window boxes tumble with colour, while inside, two open-plan sitting rooms fill with guests. Expect friendly staff, the morning papers, a bar at the front and a lift to whisk you skywards. Rooms are excellent value for money. You get waffle bathrobes, Hypnos beds, plumped-up cushions, canvas curtains. Rooms are well laid-out; some are bigger than others, but none feel cramped and you can expect a little style: crisp linen, warm reds and yellows, Somo smellies, real coffee. Breakfast, a proper continental feast (cold meats and cheese, plus the usual fare), is served in big, mirrored dining room. At night, they'll cook you a pizza and bring it to your room, but hundreds of great local restaurants are on the doorstep, including the Michelin-starred Royal China.

rooms	118: 28 singles, 30 twins, 30 doubles, 30 Grove doubles.
price	£75–£95. Singles from £65. Grove rooms £95–£120.
meals	Continental breakfast included, full English £4. Dinner £6–£15.
closed	Never.
train	Paddington (to Heathrow).
tube	Bayswater.
bus	7, 12, 94.

	Victor Phillips
tel	020 7221 9131
fax	020 7221 4073
e–mail	info@thewestminsterhotel.com
web	www.thewestminsterhotel.com

Hotel

Map 1 Entry 17

Westbourne Park Road
Westbourne Grove, London W2

This is 'the house that fell down' (it caused a stir at the time), but in true English style, Victoria not only dusted off the overalls and rebuilt, she also wrote a book about it, a copy of which is in your room. The house is all elegance, a contemporary take on its 1846 original, with pedimented windows and smart rendered walls. Inside, space flows, with huge double doors in the sitting room that open onto an airy open-plan kitchen/dining room, thus turning the ground floor into (more or less) one room. You breakfast at a large farmhouse table, with views through floor-to-ceiling French windows to a pretty garden. There are blond wooden floors, sandy colours, rooms that swim in light; very attractive. Bedrooms up on the third floor are cosy and prettily furnished. Expect oak dressers, loads of books, carafes of water, a small armchair. The room at the back is slightly bigger and can sleep three. There is also a small kitchen: you may make tea and coffee or use the microwave and washing machine. If you want to eat out, try the Cow (great food) or the Westbourne (great style). Portobello is close.

rooms	3: 1 triple with separate shower; 1 double, 1 single sharing bath (same-party bookings only).
price	£95. Singles £72. Triples £125.
meals	Continental breakfast included.
closed	Occasionally.
train	Paddington (to Heathrow).
tube	Royal Oak; Bayswater.
bus	7, 23, 27, 36.

	Uptown Reservations
tel	020 7351 3445
fax	020 7351 9383
e-mail	inquiries@uptownres.co.uk

B&B

Map 1 Entry 18

Westbourne Park Road
Westbourne Grove, London W2

A smart 1842 family home with a lush garden/jungle at the front, through which you trek to reach the front door. Sue is a picture-framer who sells old prints, and great art hangs on the walls. You pass it on the stairs as you climb up to your super bedroom. It's huge, nicely decorated in family style, with a marble fireplace, padded bedheads and exquisite Art Deco prints. You get the top floor to yourselves. There are dried flowers, a bamboo armchair and windows onto the front garden, where a London lime tree and a horse chestnut soar, offering a curtain of green to assure your privacy. Yellows and blues, books and magazines, a radio, fresh flowers and a Persian carpet. The next-door bathroom zings in 1970s blue, so bring your sunglasses. You breakfast downstairs in country-house style at a large mahogany dining table, with old rugs warming wooden floors. Outside, head north to pretty Maida Vale and its delicious canals, or stroll south to Hyde Park and the Serpentine. Try Prince Bonaparte for great pub grub, Goya for tasty tapas, or the Mandarin Kitchen for the best Chinese seafood in town.

rooms	1 twin with separate bath.
price	£95. Singles £72.
meals	Continental breakfast included.
closed	Occasionally.
train	Paddington (to Heathrow).
tube	Royal Oak; Bayswater.
bus	7, 23, 27, 36.

	Uptown Reservations
tel	020 7351 3445
fax	020 7351 9383
e-mail	inquiries@uptownres.co.uk

B&B

Map 1 Entry 19

Miller's

111a Westbourne Grove, London W2 4UW

This is Miller's, as in the antique guides, and the collectibles on show in the first-floor drawing room make it one of the loveliest rooms in this book. Breakfast is taken communally around a 1920s walnut table, while at night, cocktails are served on the house, while a fire crackles in the carved-wood fireplace and a couple of hundred candles flicker around you. It is an aesthetic overdose, exquisitely bohemian, every wall stuffed with gilt-framed pictures. An eclectic collection of regulars include movie moguls, fashion photographers, rock stars, even a professional gambler. An opera singer once gave guests singing lessons at breakfast. Wander at will and find an altar of Tibetan deities (well, their statues), a 1750s old master's chair, busts and sculptures, globes, chandeliers, plinths, rugs and a three-legged chair stuffed on top of a Regency wardrobe. Things get moved around all the time, so expect the scene to change. Muralled walls in the hall were inspired by the Pope's palace at Avignon. Bedrooms upstairs are equally embellished, just a little less cluttered. Incredible.

rooms	8: 6 doubles, 2 suites.
price	£175–£270.
meals	Continental breakfast included.
closed	Occasionally.
train	Paddington (to Heathrow).
tube	Bayswater; Queensway; Notting Hill Gate.
bus	7, 23, 28, 31, 70.

	Verginie Le Rumeur
tel	020 7243 1024
fax	020 7243 1064
e-mail	enquiries@millersuk.com
web	www.millersuk.com

Hotel

Map 1 Entry 20

Guesthouse West

163-165 Westbourne Grove, Notting Hill Gate, London W11 2RS

From the outside, this appears to be the essence of clipped English elegance, with smart black railings and an impeccable Victorian façade. Step inside and you find a cool world of smooth lines, leather sofas and light wood floors. This hotel is the new kid on the block and offers great rooms at attractive prices with Portobello on your doorstep. If you like what you see, you can buy your room on a 99-year lease; so far, 17 people have. Nomads who merely wish to pass through get a big airy sitting room/bar where all hotel life gathers. Here you can breakfast on pink grapefruit juice and natural yogurt, pick up the morning papers, and settle in for tapas and cocktails at night. Bedrooms in neutral colours are funky, with espresso coffee makers in each one, and big calming photos of a tranquil lake or a palm-fringed beach. You get sleek wood furniture, flat-screen TVs, smartly dressed beds and waffle bathrobes. There are DVD players, too (with a library at reception), and compact bathrooms that have super-cool showers. Tom Conran's deli is just across the road, and Hyde Park is a short stroll.

rooms	20 doubles.
price	£130-£160. Singles £115-£145.
meals	Breakfast £16.
	Lunch & dinner from £10.
closed	Notting Hill Carnival.
tube	Notting Hill Gate; Bayswater.
bus	7, 23, 27, 28, 70.

	Steve Head
tel	020 7792 9800
fax	020 7792 9797
e-mail	matron@guesthousewest.com
web	www.guesthousewest.com

Hotel

Map 1 Entry 21

94 Longlands Court

Portobello Road, Notting Hill Gate, London W11 2QG

This is both 'bijou' and 'chic' and if you're after a week in a cool pad on London's coolest street, you've just found it. This is a one-bedroomed self-catering flat in a small ex-council block (you'd never guess), and it's the by-product of a total renovation; only the walls survived. The inside is small but perfectly formed: a low-slung double in the tiny bedroom, a Nepalese wallhanging in the sparkling sitting room, blue and white tiles in the power-showered bathroom. You get light wood floors, Farrow & Ball paints, a glass table and padded chairs, and all the gadgetry you could want (TV, hi-fi, video). Fling open the balcony doors and watch Portobello life pass by as you polish off your breakfast. The walk-in kitchen will bring out your inner chef and there's a slimline dishwasher to do the hard work (you get all the stylish gear: stainless steel hobs and oven, fridge/freezer, washing machine/dryer). Changeover day is Friday (the market closes the street to cars on Saturdays). Notting Hill is all around – restaurants, bars, pubs, clubs – and George Orwell lived up the road, at Number 22. Sensational.

rooms	1 double.
price	£450–£550 per week.
meals	Self-catering; full kitchen facilities.
closed	Occasionally.
tube	Notting Hill Gate
bus	12, 27, 28, 31, 52, 70, 94.

Chris Finney
tel   01395 276999
fax   01395 271787
e-mail chris@varnes16.freeserve.co.uk

Self-Catering

Map 1 Entry 22

Portobello Gold
95-97 Portobello Road, Notting Hill Gate, London W11 2QB

A quirky little place bang on the Portobello Road; Bill Clinton once stopped here for a pint, then left without paying. On Saturdays the market passes directly outside, but for the rest of the week you can sit out on the pavement and watch Portobello life pass by. A very easy-going place, a cheep and cheerful sleepery where you can stay for the London equivalent of next to nothing. Rooms are basic – bed, chair, desk, TV – so if you're after fancy hotel luxury, apply elsewhere. If, however, you want to bring out your inner hippy, you'll love it here (as does a certain Alastair Sawday); the backpacker room is amazingly cheap. There's a conservatory/jungle dining room at the back (book the cushioned hippy deck), tiled floors and open fires in the bar, and good art on the walls – the place doubles as a gallery. The cyber café is free to hotel guests, there are trappist ales, Belgian beers and the best wines available by the glass (Linda is a wine writer). Superb food – Thai moules, *sashimi*, Irish rock oysters, Sunday roasts – friendly natives, and the suite has a private roof terrace, so watch the Carnival pass in August.

rooms	7: 2 doubles; 3 doubles all with shower, sharing wc; 1 backpackers twin with separate shower; 1 suite.
price	£65-£85. Twin £45. Suite £180. Singles from £45.
meals	Continental breakfast included, full English £5.50. Bar meals from £6. Lunch & dinner, £10-£25.
closed	Never.
tube	Notting Hill Gate.
bus	12, 27, 28, 31, 52, 328.

	Michael Bell & Linda Johnson-Bell
tel	020 7460 4910
fax	020 7229 2278
e-mail	reservations@portobellogold.com
web	www.portobellogold.com

Restaurant with Rooms

Map 1 Entry 23

Portobello Hotel

22 Stanley Gardens, Notting Hill Gate, London W11 2NG

The Portobello is to funky London hotels what Elvis is to rock and roll: the original. The hotel opened in 1970, a groovy response to groovy times, signalling a fundamental shift in attitudes from what was a decidedly formal world. It became *the* place to stay in London, for artists and musicians, film stars and designers – and it still is, with a star-studded list of regulars who come for its seductive combination of informality and opulence. You can sleep in a four-poster from Hampton Court Palace, refresh yourself in a brass-piped Victorian shower, recline on a curved sofa that was made to fit the room, or revitalise yourself in a steam bath. Cool, colonial interiors run throughout. Wander at will and you find ferns potted in an ancient thunder-box, a three-foot-deep gilded claw-foot bath, or Chinese sofas in a tiny dining room. The Japanese room, in bamboo and marble, has a small conservatory with doors out to a tiny courtyard garden where walls are tiled with sea shells. You can eat here or at nearby Julie's, another Notting Hill institution, owned (and cooked) by the same people. Don't miss.

rooms	24: 12 special rooms, 5 doubles, 2 twins, 5 singles.
price	£160–£185. 'Special' rooms £240–£275. Singles £140.
meals	Continental breakfast included; full English £11. Room service.
closed	23 December–3 January.
tube	Notting Hill Gate.
bus	12, 27, 28, 52, 70, 94.

Hanna Turner
tel	020 7727 2777
fax	020 7792 9641
e-mail	info@portobello-hotel.co.uk
web	www.portobello-hotel.co.uk

Hotel

Map 1 Entry 24

Campden Hill Square
Notting Hill Gate, London W8

Turner used to come and paint sunsets here, and a plaque on a tree in the communal gardens commemorates him. These grand old houses were built in the late 1820s by J F Hanson (as in the Hanson cab). They pack quite a punch, with what must have been the bare essentials of Georgian splendour: high ceilings, big windows and large rooms, all of which you get in spades. Your room, tucked away at the back, is enormous. It once had a balcony, but they knocked through, popping on a conservatory roof, which floods the place with light. There's a queen-size bed, antique silk curtains, and lots of old pine to match the double doors through which you enter. Expect fresh flowers, a pretty Provencal oil painting, porcelain vases, a collection of antique soda syphons, a shelf or two of books and a bathroom that sparkles. A second room one floor up is also available, but was occupied when I visited. Breakfast is taken downstairs in the claret-walled dining room with views out front to Susie's pretty garden. Sneak a look at her Russian submarine telephone in the kitchen; it works.

rooms	2: 1 twin/double, 1 twin.
price	£95. Singles £72.
meals	Continental breakfast included.
closed	Occasionally.
tube	Holland Park; Notting Hill Gate.
bus	12, 27, 28, 31, 52, 94.

	Uptown Reservations
tel	020 7351 3445
fax	020 7351 9383
e-mail	inquiries@uptownres.co.uk

B&B

Map 1 Entry 25

Pembridge Court

34 Pembridge Gardens, Notting Hill Gate, London W2 4DX

Splash out and go for the big rooms, which aren't big at all, but huge – and hold every conceivable object that is known to satisfy man. There are tartan sofas, high ceilings, king-size beds, thick floral curtains. The décor is warmly elegant, with an understated Victorian theme (the hotel dates to 1840); you may find a concertina fan, a pair of silk gloves or a piece of Victorian jewellery framed on the walls. There are TVs and videos, spotless bathrooms with waffle bathrobes, fluffy towels and shower heads the size of saucepan lids. Colours are warm and stylish – corals, reds, greens and yellows; one room comes grandly in black and gold. There's room service, too (salads, soups and sandwiches) and delicious cooked breakfasts in a very pretty dining room. Wander through to a cosy, peaceful sitting room at the back to find newspapers, board games, a computer that guests can use – and the BBC; they film interviews here. A very spoiling hotel, where help is given generously. Watch out for Churchill the cat; he gets his own fan mail.

rooms	20: 14 twins/doubles, 3 small singles, 3 small doubles.
price	£160–£195. Singles £125–£165.
meals	Full English breakfast included. Room Service.
closed	Never.
tube	Notting Hill Gate.
bus	12, 27, 28, 52, 70, 94.

	Nicola Green
tel	020 7229 9977
fax	020 7727 4982
e-mail	reservations@pemct.co.uk
web	www.pemct.co.uk

Hotel

Map 1 Entry 26

26 Hillgate Place
Notting Hill Gate, London W8 7ST

Hilary, an ex-lawyer, imports textiles from India, so expect a bit of glitter on the walls. These 1840 cottages were built for the poor souls who worked on the Great Western Railway (one house had a population of 33), but fortunes change and Notting Hill is now one of London's most fashionable addresses. You are bang on its doorstep, with all the local landmarks a two-minute stroll: see a movie at the Coronet, have a pint at the Windsor Castle, eat the best Thai at the Churchill. Whatever you do, roll back to Hilary's easy-going home for a bit of eastern spice. There are old teak dressers, the odd wooden elephant, wall hangings and wildly colourful art (Hilary paints). The two bedrooms are quite different. The bigger double has a Caribbean influence and is more homely (the bathroom is up a flight of stairs). The smaller double in creamy whites is smarter – immaculate, actually – and has a sofa and an enormous bathroom with a claw-foot bath and a very swanky shower. Both rooms have a small fridge and come with bathrobes. There are two gardens, one on a roof: expect palms, creepers and a fountain.

rooms	2: 1 double; 1 double sharing family bath.
price	£65-£85. Singles from £60.
meals	Continental breakfast included.
closed	Occasionally.
train	Paddington (to Heathrow).
tube	Notting Hill Gate.
bus	12, 27, 28, 31, 52, 70, 94, 328.

	Hilary Dunne
tel	020 7727 7717
fax	020 7727 7827
e-mail	hilary.dunne@virgin.net

B&B

Map 1 Entry 27

101 Abbotsbury Road
Holland Park, London W14 8EP

Holland Park is one of London's most sought-after addresses and has been for the last 400 years. Sir Walter Cope built a castle here in 1605 and called it, with breathtaking originality, Cope Castle. His son-in-law, Henry Rich, took over, became the first Earl of Holland, and changed the name to Holland House; so, not a vain bunch at all. Sunny's gorgeous family home is right opposite the park (you can birdwatch in its woods) and is well-placed. The whole top floor is generally given over to guests. Both rooms have been beautifully decorated in gentle yellows and greens, with pale green carpets, soft white duvets, pelmeted windows and a lovely, curved chest of drawers in the double bedroom. There are big porcelain table lights, an old Robert's radio, fresh flowers and treetop views. The bathroom is marble-tiled and sky-lit, with a deep cast-iron bath; great comfort is guaranteed. Breakfast is taken continental-style in the kitchen. You're near to Kensington Gardens, and the Number 9 or Number 10 bus will drop you off at the Albert Hall, Knightsbridge or Piccadilly.

rooms	2: 1 double, 1 single, sharing bath.
price	£90-£100. Singles £50.
meals	Continental breakfast included.
closed	Occasionally.
tube	Holland Park.
bus	9, 10, 12, 94.

	Sunny Murray
tel	020 7602 0179
fax	020 7602 1036
e-mail	sunny@101abb.freeserve.co.uk

B&B

Map 1 Entry 28

Holland Road
Holland Park, London W14

Charlotte is a writer whose works include a biography of Hutch, the West Indian singer. Her 1850s home is huge, with massive rooms. These houses were as grand as could be 100 years ago: this is one of the few to remain so. Lovely things all over the place: masses of cushions on the sofas in the large bay-windowed sitting room, where polished wooden floors lap against a marble fireplace, and lots of art on the walls, brought back from exotic trips. Old oils line the staircase as it curves gently upwards to gigantic bedrooms. The room at the front (some noise from the road, but it's the biggest room I've seen) has two sofas and two armchairs, though you hardly notice them, a massive old brass bed (everything is huge!), books in the bathroom, high ceilings – fabulous. At the back (therefore no noise) a canopied half-tester dominates the room – country-house living in the heart of London. You breakfast downstairs at a farmhouse table in the Aga-warmed kitchen, where doors lead out to the communal garden. A house of art, books and culture. Cibo's, the local Italian restaurant, is a treat, too.

rooms	2 doubles.
price	£95. Singles £72.
meals	Continental breakfast included, full English £5.
closed	Occasionally.
tube	Olympia; High Street Kensington; Holland Park (all a 10-minute walk).
bus	9, 10, 12, 27, 28, 49, 88.

	Uptown Reservations
tel	020 7351 3445
fax	020 7351 9383
e-mail	inquiries@uptownres.co.uk

B&B

Map 4 Entry 29

Addison Gardens
Shepherd's Bush, London W14

Not your run-of-the-mill B&B! Michael's place is wild – but when I read my notes back, I began to wonder if I'd imagined the whole thing. Gold rams? Really? Certainly a claret-and-gold crushed velvet bedcover on a French sleigh bed that's sprinkled with red cherubic cushions and flanked by stone urns that double up as bedside tables. And definitely a spiral staircase corkscrewing through the wooden floor and leading to a bathroom where the cast-iron bath stands free. Candelabra on the marble mantelpiece and gilded cornicing on the ceiling – Michael is a photographer with an eye for funky contemporary style. The room at the top is huge and has a canvas-shaded ceiling, a big sofa and a day bed in one corner. The feel is opulent: bold colours, classical pieces, lots of space, fresh flowers, piles of mags, crisp linen and rug-strewn floors. Breakfast is brought up to you: croissants and hot French bread, bowls of fruit and coffee. This vibrant area also has masses of great restaurants. Try Chinon for "outstanding" French food.

rooms	2: 1 double; 1 family with separate bath.
price	£95. Singles £72. Family £125.
meals	Continental breakfast included.
closed	Occasionally.
tube	Hammersmith; Shepherd's Bush.
bus	9, 10, 27.

	Uptown Reservations
tel	020 7351 3445
fax	020 7351 9383
e-mail	inquiries@uptownres.co.uk

B&B

Map 1 Entry 30

Sterndale Road

Brook Green, London W14 0HX

If we gave awards, we'd give one to Maggie for 'services to singles'. This is a mildly eccentric, very welcoming home-from-home for people travelling alone in the capital, and Maggie, who likes fast cars and drives an MG, pretty much gives you the run of the place. Have a sundowner in the garden, help yourself to tea and coffee, bring food home and cook a light meal at night – the cupboards and drawers in the kitchen are all labelled so you can find what you want. Guests often gather at the kitchen table in the evening and swap tales over a bottle of wine. Occasionally Rosemary, Maggie's mother, comes to stay and hosts breakfast with great flair. Spotless bedrooms are super value for money. Don't expect anything too fancy; do expect fresh flowers, padded headboards, floral curtains, painted wardrobes and trim carpets. Most have desks, and rooms at the back get the morning light. Compact bathrooms suffice. There's a sitting room downstairs packed with books where you can watch TV, or a drawing room on the first floor if you want peace and quiet. The Thames is close, too.

rooms	5: 4 singles, 1 double sharing 3 baths. Separate bathrooms by arrangement.
price	£60-£65. Singles £35-£40.
meals	Continental breakfast included.
closed	Occasionally.
tube	Hammersmith; Shepherd's Bush.
bus	9, 10, 27, 72, 220, 283, 295, 391.

	Maggie Clarke-Campbell
tel	020 7602 9768
fax	020 7603 4751
e-mail	maggiec-c@talk21.com

B&B

Map 4 Entry 31

The Upper Studio
31 Rowan Road, Brook Green, London W6 7DT

Terrific value for money in Brook Green, and close to the Thames at Hammersmith for its riverside pubs and walks. Vicky's top-floor pied-à-terre is big and airy, delightfully decorated in greens and yellows with a sofa, a padded window seat and a big twin/double bed. You also have a small kitchen (fridge, kettle, toaster, crockery) where you prepare your own continental breakfast whenever you want (it is brought up to you the night before). Also: fresh flowers, pretty floral blinds, an old bureau and a bowl of fresh fruit. Next door (you get the whole of the floor) is a lovely bathroom, with a deep cast-iron bath in which you can lie and gaze out of the skylight at passing traffic, ie. birds. So, lots of privacy, lots of style and plenty of space for those on longer stays. On the green itself, tennis courts and the Queen's Head pub with its huge garden. Nearby restaurants include: the Havelock (one of the area's most popular gastropubs) and the Pope's Eye (for carnivores). There's Gazza the dog, too.

rooms	1 twin/double.
price	£70. Singles from £50.
meals	Continental breakfast provisions left for you to prepare.
closed	Occasionally.
tube	Hammersmith.
bus	9, 10, 27.

	Vicky & Edmund Sixsmith
tel	020 8748 0930
fax	020 8741 4288
e-mail	vickysixsmith@aol.com
web	www.abetterwaytostay.co.uk

B&B

Map 4 Entry 32

The Lower Studio

31 Rowan Road, Brook Green, London W6 7DT

A magnificent basement studio, the like of which would cost a small fortune in a central London hotel. Vicky and Edmund have pulled off quite a feat. Not many people decide to excavate the foundations of their house in order to slip a contemporary designer studio underneath, but that's exactly what they've done. You will thank them for it. You get the whole place to yourself, it's huge and there's a kitchen, so if you want, you can self-cater. It is seductively cool. You get aqua-green tiles in the power shower, beds dressed in crisp white cotton and an ocean of light oak floor. Creamy curtains hang on the walls, halogen lights sparkle and you can curl up on the sofa and play with your surround-sound TV and CD/DVD player. There are fresh flowers and bathrobes, waffle bed throws and old-style radiators. Edmund is a structural engineer (he oversaw the whole project), so you can sleep easy at night. You have your own entrance, with windows on one side and pavement lights above the fully equipped kitchen (breakfast is left in the fridge). Subterranean heaven.

rooms	1 twin/double.
price	£80. Singles £60.
meals	Continental breakfast provisions left for you to prepare.
closed	Occasionally.
tube	Hammersmith.
bus	9, 10, 27.

	Vicky & Edmund Sixsmith
tel	020 8748 0930
fax	020 8741 4288
e-mail	vickysixsmith@aol.com
web	www.abetterwaytostay.co.uk

Self-Catering

Map 4 Entry 33

Dalling Road
Ravenscourt Park, London W6 0ES

Everything here is delightful. The garden waterfall was designed by medal winners at the Chelsea Flower Show, herbs grow in a Belfast sink, and one of the bedrooms has a private roof terrace. Catriona ran a PR company in Indonesia and brought back the odd souvenir (she has two container loads in storage). There are pots from Lombok, marble-topped tables, hardwood chairs… but surprisingly, the feel is of a clipped country elegance. Bedrooms come with antique wrought-iron beds, padded bedspreads, old pine dressers, silk curtains, piles of cushions and pretty mirrors. You get books everywhere (*War and Peace*, D H Lawrence), and Catriona, who has a good eye, has sprinkled the place with interesting things: towels in a glass cabinet/bedside table, jelly moulds and Hungarian goose down duvets (their geese are plumper, the feathers fluffier). Expect Osborne & Little *fleur de lys* wallpaper, summery colours, light and airy interiors. All rooms share one bathroom, but a big old shower head compensates. Breakfast is organic if possible – jams, breads and fruits. There's Magic the cat, too.

rooms	3: 2 doubles, 1 single sharing bath & shower.
price	£50-£65. Singles £35-£45.
meals	Continental breakfast included.
closed	Occasionally.
tube	Ravenscourt Park (7-minute walk).
bus	94.

Catriona & David Sinclair
tel   020 8740 5590
e-mail   catriona.sinclair@virgin.net

B&B

Map 3 Entry 34

7 Emlyn Road
Stamford Brook, London W12 9TF

This is the sort of place you see in a glossy magazine and can't quite believe is real, so let me assure you: this is one of London's loveliest B&Bs. Ricky and Sarah have lived all over the world – Upper Volta, Nicaragua, Borneo, Oman – but the influences here are homemade; this is crisp, English elegance at its best. Beautiful lighting, stencilled beds, fine English linen, original stripped-pine doors, blinds and curtains, a pretty bay window, a small balcony and an Eton burry (a desk from the school); the place is immaculate. You have two rooms, bedroom and sitting room, separated by double doors that you can throw open, thus giving yourself a great sense of space. Lots of pretty bits and bobs about the place – old books, the odd bit of art (Sarah paints), and a huge bathroom with fluffy towels. A continental breakfast is brought up to you the night before and your table set with tablecloths, napkins and fresh flowers; you then help yourself in the morning (there's even an egg-boiler). The number 94 stops at the end of the road and takes you all the way to Piccadilly; there's also the tube. A perfect ten.

rooms	1 twin/double with sitting room.
price	£75–£85. Singles from £55.
meals	Continental breakfast included.
closed	Occasionally.
tube	Stamford Brook.
bus	94.

	Sarah & Ricky Richardson
tel	020 8746 1677
e-mail	sarichardson49@yahoo.co.uk

BℰB

Map 3 Entry 35

Temple Lodge

51 Queen Caroline Street, Hammersmith, London W6 9QL

Temple Lodge, once home to the painter Sir Frank Brangwyn, is sandwiched between a courtyard and a lush half-acre garden. The peace and quiet here is remarkable, making it a very restful place – simple yet human and warmly comfortable. Michael and Heidi run it with quiet energy. There are sociable breakfasts in the vaulted basement, newspapers in the library, no TVs, and bedrooms to make you smile. Expect crisp linen and garden views. They are surprisingly stylish – clean, uncluttered with a hint of Scandinavian chic – and represent exceptional value for money. None has its own bathroom, but if that doesn't matter, you'll be delighted. The Thames passes by at the end of the road (you can follow it down to Kew) and the Riverside Studios for film and theatre is on your doorstep. The Gate Vegetarian Restaurant is closer still, 10 paces across the courtyard; it is a well-known London eatery and was Brangwyn's studio, hence the enormous artist's window. The house is a non-denominational Christian centre. There are two services a week which you may take or leave as you choose.

rooms	8: 1 double, 3 twins, 4 singles sharing 3 baths.
price	£40–£55. Singles £30.
meals	Continental breakfast included.
closed	Never.
tube	Hammersmith.
bus	9, 10, 27, 295.

	Michael Beaumont & Heidi Pedersen
tel	020 8748 8388
fax	020 8563 2758
e-mail	m.beaumont@rdplus.net

Other Place

Map 4 Entry 36

250 Lillie Road
Fulham, London SW6 7PX

An exquisite, one-bedroom, self-catering apartment with a rambling garden that doubles as a summer sitting room. You get lavender, ferns and a cherry tree, vines that yield grapes you can eat and a cushioned chair that hangs from a tree. It's not bad inside either. Step back through the French windows and you're in the big, airy open-plan kitchen/dining room. The feel is warmly contemporary, with light wood floors, creamy Farrow & Ball paints, a big well-dressed sofa, and a trendy kitchen (compact but well-equipped). The big, upstairs bedroom comes with a wall of windows that gives the impression that you are sleeping in a conservatory, while the bathroom comes in green and pink. (Nothing in this house is ordinary.) You get the whole place to yourselves, with all you need, even dishwasher and washing machine, and a cleaning lady who comes on Thursdays. The antiques shops of Fulham Cross are on the doorstep and a 10-minute walk will take you to the River Café. Very private, very stylish, very quiet, very well-priced and the antithesis of what you expect self-catering to be. *Minimum stay three nights.*

rooms	1 double.
price	£85.
meals	Self-catering; full kitchen facilites.
closed	Occasionally.
tube	Baron's Court (8-minute walk).
bus	74, 190, 211, 295.

	Linda Martin Lamb
tel	020 7385 4326
fax	020 7610 0637
e-mail	scottie250@aol.com
web	www.quietspacelondon.com

Self-Catering

Map 4 Entry 37

15 Delaford Street

Fulham, London SW6 7LT

A pretty Victorian terraced home with a choice of gardens, both small but bursting with life. One is tiny, a sun-trapping courtyard, where you can breakfast in good weather amid pots of ferns, hostas and shiny white walls. Sit on French café chairs at a marble-topped table and wolf down croissants, coffee, yogurt and exotic fruits, even smoothies – Margot is from Melbourne. The garden at the back is entered through the snug dining room (terracotta tiles, carved wood chairs, old pine farmhouse table) and here you find Virginia creeper, agapanthas and daisies mixing in with cherry blossom and invading roses from the garden next door. The bedroom, up a spiral staircase, is at the back of the house and looks down on all this. Expect pure cotton linen, a quilted throw, books in the alcove and fluffy white towels. A three-quarter bath is more than sufficient, and you'll find a TV, pot plants and plenty of storage. The tennis at Queen's is on your doorstep and takes place in the second week of June. Earl's Court and Olympia are also close. Tim and Margot are great fun and happily advise. There's Poppy the dog, too.

rooms	1 double.
price	£80. Singles £55.
meals	Continental breakfast included.
closed	Occasionally.
tube	West Brompton (10-minute walk).
bus	74, 190, 211.

	Margot & Tim Woods
tel	020 7385 9671
fax	020 7385 9671
e-mail	margotwoods@telco4u.net

B&B

Map 4 Entry 38

Hartismere Road
Fulham, London SW6 7TS

This 1880s worker's cottage is swamped in summer by a rambling Mermaid rose, soft yellow and easy on the eye. Joan is something of a globe-trotter, and the last couple of years have seen her in Namibia, Botswana, Finland, Estonia, China and by the Black Sea. Over coffee, the photo albums came out and we oohed and aahed our way around the world. She knows Fulham, too, and will tell you where to eat (Miragio's is fabulous) and what to see (the North End Road Market – more cockneys than EastEnders). You enter at the side of the house, straight into the big, open-plan kitchen/dining room, a room full of books and plants. The table here hosts what I expect are extremely convivial breakfasts, which include apple compotes, croissants and Cuban coffee, the latter a souvenir from a recent trip, so book early while stocks last. Upstairs, two bedrooms: a smallish, well-furnished double, and a delightful yellow single at the back of the house, with rugs, books and a mahogany dresser. Both have electric blankets for the odd chilly night and look onto the terraced garden, which overflows with life.

rooms	2: 1 double, 1 single sharing bath.
price	£65-£70. Singles £45-£50.
meals	Continental breakfast included.
closed	Occasionally.
tube	Fulham Broadway.
bus	14, 28, 295, 414.

	Joan Lee
tel	020 7385 0337
fax	020 7385 0337
e-mail	joan@fulhamsw.fsnet.co.uk

B&B

Map 4 Entry 39

Church Gate
Putney Bridge, London SW6

Heaven waits at Putney Bridge. This 1697 terraced house was originally part of Bishop's Palace, which stands in the park next door. It is a magical house – Grade II-listed and one of the loveliest homes in this book – yet it's Annie and Andrew that make their home shine. They are both interior designers and wherever you look, something wonderful passes the eye, be it a stone bench in the garden, a bust of Socrates in the dining room or ancient panelled walls in the sitting room. There are gilt-framed mirrors, limestone floors, thick swathes of curtain that fall from the ceiling. Delightfully, Annie and Andrew prefer to keep the feel low-key and friendly; if you want a cup of tea, just pop down and help yourself. Bedrooms are exceptional. Country-house luxury in SW6: painted panelled walls, old fireplaces, fresh flowers, fat eiderdowns, cushioned window seats, electric blankets, padded headboards, a gilt-framed bathroom mirror – stupendous stuff. In summer, the garden opens up for deliciously lazy breakfasts. Don't miss the park, the riverside walks, the Wetlands Centre. Malinda, the au pair, also helps.

rooms	3: 1 double; 1 double, 1 twin sharing bathroom (same-party bookings only).
price	£80-£85.
meals	Full English breakfast included. Dinner, 3 courses, £20.
closed	Occasionally.
tube	Putney Bridge.
bus	14, 22, 74, 414.

	The London Bed & Breakfast Agency
tel	020 7586 2768
fax	020 7586 6567
e-mail	stay@londonbb.com

B&B

Map 4 Entry 40

6 Grimston Road

Hurlingham, London SW6 3QP

A divine house; you walk under a rose arbour to get to the front door. Inside, the very essence of crisp country elegance. There are painted wood floors, Louis XV armchairs, marble-topped tables, a Venetian glass mirror, a sparkling chandelier. Gilly used to work at Christie's (a copy of his portrait hangs on the wall) and her house is full of beautiful things. You breakfast at an ancient French oak table in an open-plan kitchen/dining room while sitting on old church chairs. Bedrooms upstairs are not big, but delightfully furnished with gilt-framed mirrors, pretty art, *toile de Jouy* fabrics, Farrow & Ball paints. Beds are comfy, well-dressed and have padded headboards. One room has delicate voile curtains and painted wood floors, the room in the eaves swims in crisp light. Very pretty, nice and restful, carafes of water, excellent bathrooms. There's tennis at Hurlingham in the second week of June, or head for the Centre Court at Wimbledon (Gilly will happily drop you off). The tube is a three-minute walk; alternatively, hop on the Number 22 and head for Chelsea, Knightsbridge, Piccadilly.

rooms	3: 1 twin/double, 1 single; 1 double with separate bath.
price	£75. Singles £50.
meals	Full English breakfast included.
closed	Occasionally.
tube	Putney Bridge.
bus	14, 22, 74.

	Gilly Belfrage
tel	020 7731 1193
e-mail	g.belfrage@talk21.com

B&B

Map 4 Entry 41

Cassocks House

81 Peterborough Road , Fulham, London SW6 3BU

A late-Victorian red-brick house with a lovely parterre garden to the front, where rosemary and lavender bloom in summer. Mary has been doing B&B for 12 years and her home is spotless and quietly stylish: original tiled floors in the hall, good prints and comfy sofas in the guest sitting room, Fortnum & Mason china and red silk curtains in the dining room. Come down to breakfast and find the papers waiting, then feast on fine sausages, smoked bacon, eggs any way you want them. Bedrooms are simply furnished with excellent basics: padded headboards, trim carpets, Jane Churchill linen, red and orange check blankets. Not a speck of dust, but a daily maid service just in case, with fresh towels every day if you want them. The twin at the back has a large bathroom with a small bunk-bedded room next door, making it perfect for families; Mary, a grandmother, has high chairs, travel cots and a pushchair (stroller) which you are free to borrow. Up on the top floor two more exceptionally bright rooms wait. The single in the eaves has a low-slung bed and the twin has long views towards the centre of town.

rooms	4: 2 twins, 1 single, 1 room with bunkbeds for children.
price	£75. Singles £55. Families (1 twin, bunk beds) £100.
meals	Full English breakfast included.
closed	Occasionally.
tube	Parsons Green
bus	22.

	Mary Laurie
tel	020 7736 2617
e-mail	mary@cassockshouse.co.uk
web	www.cassockshouse.co.uk

B&B

Map 4 Entry 42

3 Bradbourne Street
Fulham, London SW6 3TF

This B&B has passed from mother to daughter, so come and witness the birth of a dynasty. Lucy and Charlie are perfect for it: warm and generous, in the know, easy-going and utterly committed. They are also eager to put their stamp on the place: rooms were being painted, bathrooms put in and space found on the walls to hang their paintings. All this activity despite the arrival of a long-term guest (their first baby). Two rooms for B&B come in the shape of a lower-ground double (big and bright, warm and airy, excellent for longer stays) and a first-floor twin that overlooks the garden, newly decorated. Breakfast is served in the open-plan kitchen/dining room, but moves outside to the courtyard garden in good weather. Expect good coffee, hot croissants, pains au chocolate and fresh fruit. This handsome 1880s red-brick home stands just around the corner from the New King's Road and less than a minute's walk from Parsons Green. Stroll across it and you come to the famous White Horse pub, where you can eat and drink like a king. A great little place, a home-from-home in the city.

rooms	2: 1 twin/double, 1 double, both with separate bath.
price	£80. Singles £55.
meals	Continental breakfast included.
closed	Rarely.
tube	Parsons Green.
bus	22.

Charlie & Lucy Smith
tel	020 7736 7284
e-mail	bookings@bradbournestreet.com
web	www.bradbournestreet.com

B&B

Map 4 Entry 43

49 Quarrenden Street

Parsons Green, London SW6 3ST

There's a Bible box in the dining room, probably something to do with Gudrin's sinful breakfasts. This is a very comfortable house – smart, homely, welcoming – and Gudrin looks after you in style. Up in the eaves, there are two pretty doubles (draped bedheads, an ornate French bed, pine dressers, an old armoire), perfect for families as they share a bathroom. One flight down and the single in blue has a cane sofa and good storage, while the double at the front is the biggest room, with ragged yellow walls, an old dresser, a marble-topped table and silk roses. The fabrics are plush, the bed is large, gilt mirrors hang on the wall. It is entirely civilised: not old-fashioned, rather timelessly elegant, and airy and bright. There are good pictures as you climb the stairs – country scenes on your way to the first floor, old maps on the next flight up. Back downstairs, Rosenthal Christmas plates add colour to dining room walls. As for breakfast, expect a feast – the whole cooked works, cold meats and cheese, cereal and toast… and chocolate biscuits. There's a small garden, yours in summer, and Gypsy, the King Charles spaniel.

rooms	4: 1 twin/double; 2 doubles sharing bath; 1 single sharing bath.
price	£60-£75. Singles £40.
meals	Full English breakfast included.
closed	Occasionally.
tube	Parsons Green
bus	22.

Gudrin Richards
tel   020 7731 0821

B&B

Map 4 Entry 44

Stokenchurch Street

Parsons Green, London SW6 3TR

This is a warm and friendly home – nicely stylish, nothing too cluttered – and Jennie works hard to make guests happy. The emphasis here is on excellent basics: super-comfortable beds, crisp linen, the odd antique and hearty breakfasts. This 1880s red-brick house was recently renovated and sparkles in mellow yellow. Follow your nose and find pretty prints on the walls, halogen spotlighting, fresh flowers and carafes of water in every room. The top floor has two rooms that share a bathroom and is excellent for families. Expect warm colours, antique dressers, thick blankets, pretty rugs, loads of mirrors. Tea and coffee is brought up to your room, you can have sheets or duvets, and if you're allergic, they've got an alternative. Bathrooms are excellent, too, with deep cast-iron baths, and two have Grohr showers (the best, apparently). Breakfast, a feast, is served in the dining room, where an impressive window of arches and squares floods the place with morning light; beyond, smart pots of topiary line the sills. Great service given generously with a real smile.

rooms	5: 1 double, 1 twin/double sharing bath; 1 single, 1 double sharing bath; 1 twin/double with separate bath.
price	£65–£75. Singles £45–£55.
meals	Full English breakfast included.
closed	Never.
tube	Fulham Broadway.
bus	11, 22, 28, 295.

Jennie Butler

tel	020 7731 2281
fax	020 7731 2281
e-mail	clive@butler650.fsnet.co.uk

B&B

Map 4 Entry 45

8 Parthenia Road

Fulham, London SW6 4BD

A smart London-brick house, hidden at the front by a well-trimmed box hedge that George keeps in fine order. Your room is at the top of the house: four short flights of stairs await, but your reward is well worth the effort as you find a sumptuous room, decorated beautifully in country-house style (Caroline is an interior designer). You get an old oak table, a plush armchair, wonderfully heavy curtains, the crispest linen, carafes of water – heavenly stuff. There's loads of storage space and a pretty shower room, though if you'd like a bath, one can be arranged. The whole house is crammed with beautiful art; the journey up and down the stairs is like wandering through an art gallery. Down at the bottom you get breakfast at the old oak table in the dining room, where portraits of a couple of ancestors hang on the walls. There's a small, pretty brick garden, where you can have your croissants and coffee, a delight on fine mornings. Caroline mixes the sophistication of the city with the human warmth of the countryside – this is a great place to stay. The King's Road boutiques and antiques are close by.

rooms	1 twin/double.
price	£80-£100.
meals	Continental breakfast included.
closed	Rarely.
tube	Parsons Green.
bus	14, 22.

	Caroline & George Docker
tel	020 7384 1165
fax	020 7371 8819
e-mail	carolined@angelwings.co.uk

B&B

Map 4 Entry 46

Delvino Road

Parsons Green, London SW6

There are bay trees at the front door, while inside Lottie, the King Charles spaniel, roams without malice. Your hostess runs a smooth ship and gives more than you'd expect; rooms are cleaned everyday and airport pick-ups can be arranged. The house is clutter-free. Bedrooms have a simple elegance: cane bedheads, pastel colours, the odd desk, piles of magazines, an armchair if there's space. The big room up in the eaves floods with light, while the twin overlooks the garden at the back. There are clocks and heaters, thermos flasks of fresh milk and bottles of mineral water. There are crumpets for breakfast – reason enough to come – and you can wash them down with gallons of English tea or French coffee; if you want a croissant, one will appear from the oven, piping hot. In summer, you can take your coffee into the garden and sit amid flowering tropical plants. Parsons Green is at the end of the road. Don't miss the White Horse for great food and some of the best-kept beers in Europe. There's a fair on the green in early July, a bit of old-fashioned fun that brings out the locals in droves.

rooms	4: 2 twins; 1 twin, 1 single sharing bath & shower (same-party bookings only).
price	£60–£70. Singles £40–£45
meals	Continental breakfast included.
closed	Occasionally.
tube	Parsons Green.
bus	14, 22, 414.

tel	020 7736 5648

B&B

Map 4 Entry 47

Elmstone Road

Parsons Green, London SW6

A sparkling home. Peter and Jenny are old hands at receiving guests, though you'd never guess, so easy is their way. They gave their 1895 terraced house a complete makeover a few years back, a seven-month overhaul that saw the import of great comforts, not least the bathrooms, which shine in Spanish and Italian marble. Their home is cosy and stylish – warm colours, old oil paintings, a grandfather clock – and colourful bedrooms have been carefully thought out. You'll find crisp sheets and woollen blankets, gilt mirrors, lots of books, pretty art and jugs of iced water. No clutter – everything is just so and utterly spotless, with trim carpets, smart fabrics and big fluffy towels. A few surprises wait, not least the photograph albums on the landing – a gallery of kings and the odd field marshal (Jenny is a descendant of Haig). Breakfast is a feast – Peter scrambles the eggs, Jenny sizzles the bacon, the marmalade is homemade and the coffee comes fresh from the pot. Peter will fill you in on what to do, how to get there (the tube is a two-minute walk), and the restaurants of the Fulham Road are a short stroll.

rooms	2: 1 double, 1 twin.
price	£80–£85. Singles £55–£60.
meals	Full English breakfast included.
closed	Occasionally.
tube	Parsons Green.
bus	14, 22, 414.

tel	020 7586 2768
fax	020 7586 6567
e-mail	stay@londonbb.com

B&B

Map 4 Entry 48

21 Barclay Road
Fulham, London SW6 1EJ

Paradise for music lovers in SW6. Charlotte's grand piano is a magnet for opera singers, esteemed conductors and music professors from around the world, and visiting musicians are welcome to stay and practice here. Charlotte, a Bostonian at home in London, does something unspeakably high-powered by day, then hits the keyboard at night to unwind. She is great fun – relaxed and relaxing – and she plays splendidly (Cole Porter, Noel Coward); some evenings recitals are held in the big, airy sitting room. You pretty much get the run of the house, making this a very special place to stay. Expect a private sitting room (open fire, leather sofa, loads of London guides), and a smallish double bedroom next door, with picket-fenced window boxes on the ledge, fresh flowers, seagrass matting and William Morris fabrics. There are waffle bathrobes, a bathroom that looks like a library, and two roof terraces, one at tree-top level for lazy sundowners. Breakfast is a feast, with delicious homemade cranberry muffins, French toast, smoked bacon and good coffee. A very easy-going place and a great London find.

rooms	1 double with separate bathroom. 1 single available on request. Use of grand piano, by arrangement.
price	£80. Singles £55.
meals	Continental Breakfast included.
closed	Occasionally.
tube	Fulham Broadway.
bus	14, 28, 295.

	Charlotte Dexter
tel	020 7384 3390
fax	020 7384 3390
e-mail	info@barclayhouselondon.com
web	www.barclayhouselondon.com

B&B

Map 4 Entry 49

Walham Grove
Fulham, London SW6

These 1850 houses were built for country gentlemen who needed a small pad in the city. By 'small' they clearly meant 'large' for these are big old houses, light and airy, with grand high ceilings, intricate cornicing and double doors. The outside is formal (smart brick façade, racing-green front door, cascading colour from window boxes), but step inside and you find an easy-going elegance. There are Zoffany fabrics, swathes of plush curtain, gilt-framed mirrors and enormous sofas (you are encouraged to sink in). Bedrooms upstairs are dreamy. Clifford is an interior designer, so expect controlled flamboyance. Walls are ragged in greens or apricots, there are big padded headsteads, draped curtains, pretty John Lewis linen and lovely prints. Tartan blankets cover the beds, bathrobes hang on the doors; you even get an A-Z. As for the bathroom, pure heaven. There's a huge bath, soft limestone tiles, an Art Deco mirror and a power shower to beat all power showers. You breakfast in a warmly cosy kitchen/dining room and doors open onto a small garden, where the tortoise (Nikki Lauder) roams.

rooms	2 doubles sharing bath & shower (same-party bookings only).
price	£95. Singles £72.
meals	Continental breakfast included.
closed	Occasionally.
train	West Brompton (Gatwick airport).
tube	Fulham Broadway
bus	11, 14, 28, 211, 295, 391, 414.

	Uptown Reservations
tel	020 7351 3445
fax	020 7351 9383
e-mail	inquiries@uptownres.co.uk

B&B

Map 4 Entry 50

Twenty Nevern Square
Earl's Court, London SW5 9PD

A smart red-brick exterior with terracotta urns guarding the steps and an arched porch at the front door. This is a great place, a fusion of classical and minimalist styles, with a clean, cool contemporary interior and beautiful things all around: Victorian birdcages, gilt mirrors, porcelain vases, a bowl full of dried rose petals. There's a real flow to the downstairs, all the way though to the conservatory-bar, with its stained glass, ceiling fans, cane chairs and glass tables. Bedrooms are equally stylish, with natural colours on the walls, cedar-wood blinds and rich fabrics throughout: silks, cottons and linens – nothing here is synthetic. CD players and TVs have been cleverly hidden away in pretty wooden cabinets; there is no clutter. Rooms come in different shapes and sizes, each with something to elate: an Indonesian hand-carved wooden headboard, an Egyptian sleigh bed, a colonial four-poster, some sweeping blue and gold silk curtains. A couple of the rooms have balconies, there are marble bathrooms, too. An open fire warms the sitting room in winter. Good value for money, very friendly staff, and close to the tube.

rooms	20: 13 doubles, 3 twins, 1 suite, 3 four-posters.
price	£99–£140. Four-posters from £120. Suite from £190. Singles £80–£110.
meals	Continental breakfast included, full English £5–£7.
closed	Never.
tube	Earl's Court.
bus	74, 328.

	Sadik Saloojee
tel	020 7565 9555
fax	020 7565 9444
e-mail	hotel@twentynevernsquare.co.uk
web	www.twentynevernsquare.co.uk

Hotel

Map 4 Entry 51

The Mayflower Hotel

26-28 Trebovir Road, Earl's Court, London SW5 9NJ

The Mayflower is simply amazing, a steal of a hotel that gives great style at knockdown prices with no catches. Harry's Bar in New York was the inspiration for the interior of the juice bar, while in reception an enormous wood carving from Jaipur frames a sculpted waterfall. Wander at will and come across creamy stone floors, leather sofas, American walnut and original art. Bedrooms are not huge but wonderfully designed, with shiny red marble bathrooms and exceptional walk-in showers. Most are filled with unusual antiques from India and the Far East, with lots of carved wood, gorgeous Andrew Martin fabrics and light wood floors. You get swish curtains, Merino wool blankets, Egyptian cotton and ceiling fans. The technology is state-of-the-art, the use of space is clever. Rooms at the front flood with light and a couple have balconies. Family rooms are super-funky with bunk beds and good lighting. The tube is a two-minute walk and Earl's Court is on your doorstep. Don't miss the Troubadour for live music and great food; Bob Dylan, Jimi Hendrix and Joni Mitchell all played here in the 60s.

rooms	47: 28 doubles, 11 twins, 3 singles, 5 family.
price	£89. Singles £59-£79. Family £120.
meals	Continental breakfast included, full English £5-£10.
closed	Never.
tube	Earl's Court.
bus	74, 328.

	Faisal Saloojee
tel	020 7370 4934
fax	020 7370 0994
e-mail	info@mayflower-group.co.uk
web	www.mayflowerhotel.co.uk

Hotel

Map 4 Entry 52

Amsterdam Hotel
7 Trebovir Road, Earl's Court, London SW5 9LS

The Amsterdam is a good find, tucked away in an Earl's Court back street, close to the tube. It is very well-priced and absolutely spotless, with an army of maids who blitz it daily, top to toe. Another boon is the size of the bedrooms: either big or fairly big. Some are highly idiosyncratic, decorated in bright, bold colours (yellow and blue, purple and orange, blue and green), while others are more contemporary with off-white walls, light wood floors, wicker furniture and thick rugs. There are good bathrooms, not huge, but entirely adequate, ample lighting, sofas or armchairs in every room. Singles all have double beds and the triples and family rooms are great value for money. Judith, who runs the place with real spirit, does all the upholstery herself, an incredible feat. A very pretty garden at the back basks in summer sun, so bring back a picnic or a bottle of wine. There's internet access, lots of mirrors on the walls, and a pretty yellow breakfast room with wooden floors. A very friendly place. Earl's Court is at the end of the road, as is the tube.

rooms	27: 9 twins/doubles, 4 singles, 6 family, 8 suites.
price	£88-£98. Family rooms £112-£125. Singles from £78. Suites £110-£160.
meals	Continental breakfast included, full English £3.
closed	Never.
tube	Earl's Court.
bus	74, 328.

	Judith Verrier
tel	020 7370 2814
fax	020 7244 7608
e-mail	enquiries@amsterdam-hotel.com
web	www.amsterdam-hotel.com

Hotel

Map 4 Entry 53

6 Oakfield Street
Little Chelsea, London SW10 9JB

Margaret and Simon take it in turns to cook breakfast at the weekends so they can each be sure of a lie-in! This district dates from the mid-1660s and Simon, who knows his Chelsea onions, has maps to prove it. He can tell you where Queen Elizabeth I sheltered from the rain, or where Sir Thomas More lived. He also makes delightfully eccentric collages that hang on the walls. Enter their 1860s house and you glimpse a collection of Egyptian prints – they once lived in Cairo. There's an open-plan feel to the kitchen, a marble-topped table in the dining room, and a second-floor roof terrace where you can sit in summer under a smart green umbrella. You can have bacon and eggs for breakfast, then hop on the Number 14 bus to Piccadilly – perfect; they also do a mean cup of coffee. Bedrooms are at the top of the house. The twin, in blue and yellow, is smaller than the double, but being at the back is silent at night. The double has a big wooden bed and an 18th-century oak armoire. Restaurants on Hollywood Road are a 30-second stroll and close by is Brompton Cemetery, well worth discovering.

rooms	2: 1 double, 1 twin.
price	£70. Singles £50.
meals	Full English breakfast included.
closed	Occasionally.
tube	Earl's Court (15-minute walk).
bus	14.

	Margaret & Simon de Maré
tel	020 7352 2970
e-mail	demare@easynet.co.uk

Off Cheyne Walk

Chelsea, London SW3

An extraordinary house. Walk through the front door and a sense of history is palpable; 300-year-old panelling surrounds you and it runs thoughout the house. It is grand, yet warm – a country house in SW3. In the basement there's a sand-blasted beam and a chandelier under which you breakfast at a fine mahogany table. Up a couple of flights of stairs and you come to an airy first-floor drawing room with comfy sofas, big gilt mirrors and alcoves jammed with books. Next door, one bedroom comes with a wrought-iron bed that is covered in pretty linen and a red and white check woollen blanket. There are shuttered windows, an original fireplace, rugs on the floor, bathrobes hanging from the bathroom door. Keep climbing upwards, past an ancient window seat, turn right at the rocking horse and enter another delicious room. This one has a French wooden bed and connects with a second twin, thus ideal for families. You get a sloping floor, a TV in the fireplace, lots of mirrors and an armchair. The King's Road is close, as is the Cross Keys for excellent pub grub.

rooms	3: 1 double; 1 twin, 1 double sharing bath (same party bookings only).
price	£95. Singles £72.
meals	Continental breakfast included, full English £5.
closed	Occasionally.
tube	South Kensington; Sloane Square (both a 10-minute-walk).
bus	11, 19, 22, 49, 211.

	Uptown Reservations
tel	020 7351 3445
fax	020 7351 9383
e-mail	inquiries@uptownres.co.uk

B&B

Map 4 Entry 55

Old Church Street
Chelsea, London SW3

If you see the dining room first, you'll want to camp in it! It is panelled on all sides – old ship's timber that predate this Grade II, 1914, Arts-and-Crafts-style house by a couple of hundred years – rare in a London home. There's also a rather grand oil on the wall (Clair, the owner, will tell you of whom) and a screen by the window to protect you from passing eyes while you eat your cornflakes. The rest of the house is more contemporary: shiny wooden floors, arched windows, white walls, a "family throne", and, on the first floor, a music room, with a harp and a grand piano. The bedroom is at the front of the house and has a king-size double and a single bed. It's a big room with rugs on a wooden floor, crisp linen, two armchairs and lots of mirrors. A glorious bathroom waits next door, decorated with blue-green mosaics. You're in the middle of Chelsea, a minute from the King's Road, or you can walk across Albert Bridge and be in Battersea Park in under 10. Good pubs and restaurants are close by: try the ever-popular Cross Keys, or the Angelsea with its pavement table and chairs.

rooms	1 family.
price	£95. Singles £72. Triples £125.
meals	Continental breakfast included, full English £5.
closed	Occasionally.
tube	Sloane Square (15-minute walk).
bus	11, 19, 22, 49, 211, 319.

	Uptown Reservations
tel	020 7351 3445
fax	020 7351 9383
e-mail	inquiries@uptownres.co.uk

B&B

Map 4 Entry 56

Elm Park Gardens
Chelsea, London SW3

A turn-of-the-century mansion block just behind the Chelsea Arts Club, with a large, plush bedroom and access to one of those big communal gardens so adored by the lucky Londoners that have them. Maggie, a fitness instructor, serves breakfast (pains au chocolat, croissants, fruit, the odd organic egg) in a mediterranean-style conservatory, where doors lead out to the terracotta pots of a small private garden. The big, bright bedroom at the back of the house (more garden views) is spotless. You'll find crisp linen, orange woollen blankets, halogen lighting and cushions piled up on the bed. Best of all is the fabulous marble bathroom with deep bath, a wall of mirror, big white towels, heated towel rails and "the most powerful shower ever," to quote a hundred former guests. Maggie and Peter are easy-going, keen for you to have as much privacy as you please. They know the area well and will advise you, but you're between the Fulham Road and the King's Road, so you can pretty much follow your nose and not get lost. Good antique shops are close by as is the Anglesea pub, for great food.

rooms	1 double.
price	£95. Singles £72.
meals	Continental breakfast included.
closed	Occasionally.
tube	Gloucester Road (12-minute walk).
bus	11, 14, 19, 22, 211, 319, 345.

	Uptown Reservations
tel	020 7351 3445
fax	020 7351 9383
e-mail	inquiries@uptownres.co.uk

B&B

Map 4 Entry 57

Blakes Hotel

33 Roland Gardens, South Kensington, London SW7 3PF

Blakes is unique – a work of art, not merely a hotel. It is an explosion of creativity. Leave the colonial magnificence of the airy honeymoon suite (15-foot-high four-poster bed, stencilled walls, mother-of-pearl dressers, painted wood floors) for the sinful opulence of the Cardinal's Room (Catholic blacks and reds, golden embroidery, oils by the score, a domed bathroom). Everywhere there is something delightful, be it walls of old tomes in the library suite, a tented Ottoman in black and gold, Victorian bird cages in reception, or the shaded fifth-floor roof terrace. Plump cushions by the dozen lie heaped upon beds, scented candles burn in each room. There are Art Deco mirrors, handmade beds, muralled bathrooms, exquisite prints. Vintage Louis Vitton trunks double as coffee tables, gilded rams' heads are carved into a four-poster. Tear yourself away and discover a peaceful garden at the back where lanterns hang from the trees – or head to the bar for cocktails and a chat. We haven't really scratched the surface. Magnificent.

rooms	48: 17 singles, 19 doubles, 3 twins, 9 suites.
price	£305-£405. Singles from £170. Suites from £665.
meals	Breakfast £17.50-£25. Lunch £25. Dinner £75.
closed	Never.
tube	Gloucester Road; South Kensington.
bus	14, 49, 211.

	Anouska Hempel
tel	020 7370 6701
fax	020 7373 0442
e-mail	blakes@blakeshotels.com
web	www.blakeshotels.com

Hotel

Map 4 Entry 58

The Cranley Hotel

10 Bina Gardens, South Kensington, London SW5 0LA

In a charming quiet London street of brightly painted Georgian houses, the Cranley has a neat front garden with wooden tables and chairs, clipped bay trees and wide steps up to the front door. The hall leads straight into a calm drawing room with deep Wedgewood-blue walls, original fireplaces, good antiques, coir carpets and the odd lively rug. Bedrooms are extremely comfortable: pale carpets, lilac walls, embroidered headboards over huge beds, plain cream curtains with bedspreads to match, pretty windows and cream-tiled snazzy bathrooms. Robes and slippers, state-of-the-art technology, air conditioning, prettily-laid tables for continental breakfast if you don't want it in bed and lovely Penhaligon smellies as a link back to the family who once owned the house. A cream tea with warm scones and clotted cream in the afternoon comes with the package, along with champagne and canapés at 7pm before you go off to an excellent local restaurant booked by the friendly staff. A treasure. *Weekend rates from £145, breakfast included.*

rooms	39: 4 singles, 15 doubles, 10 twins, 9 four-posters, 1 suite.
price	£210-£225. Four-posters £260. Suite £345. Singles £180.
meals	Continental breakfast £9.95. 24-hour room service.
closed	Never.
tube	South Kensington; Gloucester Road.
bus	49, 70, 345.

	Robert Wauters
tel	020 7373 0123
fax	020 7373 9497
e-mail	info@thecranley.com
web	www.thecranley.com

Hotel

Map 4 Entry 59

Kensington House Hotel

15-16 Prince of Wales Terrace, Kensington, London W8 5PQ

Kensington House dates to 1875 and its pedimented windows have Prince of Wales feathers woven into their design. This is a smart yet informal hotel (old-fashioned service, new-fangled gadgets) and the style is contemporary and colourful – sympathetic minimalism. Wind up the original staircase and you pass the odd piece of contemporary art; cane armchairs and a bowl of apples on the landing, black and white photos on the walls. Rooms have a cool colonial feel (ceiling fans, shiny wood floors, plantation blinds) and those at the front have beautiful high windows that fill the room with crisp light. You get red leather armchairs, stainless steel lamps, waffle bathrobes, the odd oriental statue. Beds are wooden, bathrooms are marble, and one of the singles has a private balcony. The higher you get, the better the view, and right at the top, snug rooms up in the eaves are nicely cosy. Breakfast in the dining room/bar with the morning papers, then return in the evening for a cocktail or a bite to eat. A very friendly place, with good service from committed staff. *Weekend rates available.*

rooms	41: 11 singles, 28 twins/doubles, 2 suites.
price	£175-£195. Singles £150. Suites £215.
meals	Continental breakfast included. Lunch & dinner £5-£25.
closed	Never.
tube	Gloucester Road; Kensington High Street.
bus	9, 10, 49, 52, 70.

	Samantha Fitzgerald
tel	020 7937 2345
fax	020 7368 6700
e-mail	reservations@kenhouse.com
web	www.kenhouse.com

Hotel

Map 1 Entry 60

The Attic

19 Palace Gate, Kensington, London W8 5LS

You get a bit of rock 'n' roll at the Attic. Step out of the tiny antique lift and enter a funky wonderland, where pop art jostles with red leather armchairs and one of the walls is covered in gold leaf. There's cutting-edge gadgetry to satisfy your every whim, with a music system that runs throughout the flat (listen to your favourite tunes while being doused in a three-sided jet shower), a plasma-screen TV and an amplifier, so bring your electric guitar. Bronze and silver leaf walls in Arabic-style conceal secret doors that lead to a classically-inspired bedroom: a Florentine chandelier, a gilded dressing table, doors that open onto a small balcony, where flowers flourish in stone urns. Head upstairs to the roof terrace, the real surprise. Amid wandering jasmine and passion flower, and overlooked by a statue of Buddha to keep the karma cool, you find a hot tub in which to soak while you gaze across a sublime London skyline (Natural History Museum, Hyde Park); there's a sauna, too, with glass doors, so you don't lose the view. Breakfast is from a local deli; yoga teachers can be arranged. Out of this world.

rooms	1 double.
price	£140.
meals	Continental breakfast at local deli included.
closed	Occasionally.
tube	High Street Kensington; Gloucester Road.
bus	9, 10, 49, 52, 70.

	Pushaun Choudhury
tel	020 7460 4454
fax	020 7460 4462
e-mail	info@theatticlondon.com
web	www.theatticlondon.com

B&B

Map 1 Entry 61

De Vere Gardens
Kensington, London W8

An impeccable house in every way. Kensington Palace is at the end of the road, Hyde Park is pretty much your garden and the Albert Hall is a short stroll. Inside, you get pampered in stately fashion, which may account for the *petonkas*, Zimbabwean wooden seats on which tribal elders sit to smoke clan pipes. This is a lower-ground apartment in a smart mansion block and you get the back of it to yourself. The bedroom is quite some treat, with a wall of windows that look onto a very pretty courtyard garden of ivy, bamboo and tumbling ferns. You get the impression you are almost sleeping in a conservatory, albeit a very private one. Expect marble bedside tables, smartly dressed armchairs, gilt mirrors, Roman blinds, high ceilings, loads of storage space and an Indonesian frieze carved in wood on one wall. There's a TV and hi-fi, but if you prefer peace and quiet, you will have it. This relatively youthful street was built in 1875 on the site of a horse-and-cart race track. Famous past residents include Robert Browning (No 29) and Henry James (No 34). Don't miss Bellini's, a very friendly local Italian.

rooms	1 double with separate bath.
price	£95. Singles £72.
meals	Continental breakfast included.
closed	Occasionally.
tube	High Street Kensington; Gloucester Road.
bus	9, 10, 49, 52, 70.

	Uptown Reservations
tel	020 7351 3445
fax	020 7351 9383
e-mail	inquiries@uptownres.co.uk

B&B

Map 1 Entry 62

Hyde Park Gate
Kensington, London SW7 5DH

Winston Churchill lived in this street, as did Epstein, while Virginia Woolfe grew up in this actual house (now five flats). This illustrious hall of fame has much to do with the position of the road, a cul-de-sac on the Knightsbridge/Kensington border, a one-minute stroll from Kensington Gardens. Walk to the end of the road (30 seconds), pick up the No 9 bus and let it chauffeur you to Piccadilly. Your room sits quietly at the back, sweetly decorated in corals, with a compact yet sparkling shower room. You get cut flowers, fruit and chocolates, fresh milk and proper china. There's lots of space, books and magazines, a TV, too, and your private loo doubles as a library. As for breakfast, Jasmyne spoils you rotten. You get the full works (or smoked salmon and scrambled eggs on Sundays), served on smart china by the window at a mahogany dining table. Lots of good restaurants nearby, and, if you want, you can walk through parks all the way to Buckingham Palace, Westminster, Oxford Street or Notting Hill. Great stuff.

rooms	1 double.
price	£75. Singles £55.
meals	Full English breakfast included.
closed	Occasionally.
tube	High Street Kensington; Gloucester Road.
bus	9, 10, 52.

	Jasmyne Davoudi
tel	020 7584 9404

B&B

Map 4 Entry 63

The Gore
190 Queens Gate, Kensington, London SW7 5EX

To those who know it, there is nowhere else to stay in London. Run with great charm by Peter McKay, an old-school hotelier who likes a little glamour, the Gore is decidedly English – a gentleman's club for those on the hop. Step in off the street and you'll think you've entered a gallery. Oil paintings cover the walls (there are 5,000 in the hotel), a graceful chandelier glistens, the odd Doric column looms, and potted palms flourish. A rich, Victorian interior comes with an overdose of colour: expect smart Oriental carpets, gilt-framed mirrors, draped silk curtains, panelled walls. Bedrooms are extravagantly furnished with antique beds, old oak chests, marble busts and mahogany dressers. One room is a genuine Tudor fake, with original 1500s panelling and a vaulted roof; another has a mirrored bathroom and faux-leopard-skin upholstery. Back downstairs, there's a panelled local's bar for cocktails, a country-house drawing room for the morning papers and an airy bistro in yellow with pictures stuffed on the walls. The Albert Hall is just around the corner and Kensington Gardens is at the end of the road.

rooms	53: 27 doubles, 20 singles, 6 suites.
price	£225-£250. Singles £180. Suites £340.
meals	Breakfast £10.95-£16.95. Lunch from £15. Dinner from £40. Pre-theatre menu £25.
closed	Never.
tube	Gloucester Road; South Kensington.
bus	9, 10, 52, 70.

	Alex McEwen
tel	020 7584 6601
fax	020 7589 8127
e-mail	reservations@gorehotel.com
web	www.gorehotel.co.uk

Hotel

Map 1 Entry 64

central

- **Hyde Park:** bikes, kites, horses, deckchairs, picnics and Speaker's Corner
- **St James's Park:** serene restaurant overlooks the lake - a sanctuary for birds
- **Trafalgar Square:** Nelson's Column, National Gallery, National Portrait Gallery, pigeons
- **Houses of Parliament; Big Ben; St Paul's; Tower of London**
- **British Museum; Museum of London; Royal Academy; Courtauld Galleries; Tate Britain**
- **Horse Guards Parade** (Trooping the Colour in June)
- **West End for cinemas and theatres; Soho** for gay bars, Chinese food and Ronnie Scott's (jazz)
- **Oxford Street, Regent Street and Piccadilly** (Selfridges, Liberty, Fortnum & Mason);

  Bond Street and Sloane Street (designer stores);

  Knightsbridge (Harrods, Harvey Nichols); **Marylebone High Street** (charming shops and delis);

  Covent Garden (shops, buskers, open-air cafés)

Off Kensington Road
Knightsbridge, London SW7

Just about everything in this delectable home is Welsh, including Mary, who is far too kind to those lucky souls who wash up at her smart Knightsbridge doorstep. To get to it, you either take the lift or navigate your way up one floor in this Art Deco mansion block (chrome banister rails, marble floors and trim rugs) that's a little like a 1920s P&O steamer; quietly grand. Once inside you find the following, all Welsh: antique china, a beautiful dresser, a Regency rosewood dining table for breakfast by the window, and the loveliest linen. Much, too, that has no declared nationlity: wild Zoffany wallpaper, old oils on the walls, a pristine marble fireplace and rugs on the floors. Very pretty windows wrap around the flat, flooding it with light. The bedroom is equally lovely (a Louis XIV sofa, wicker bedside tables, big porcelain lamps, fresh flowers) with double doors that open onto a tiny balcony, and a wonderfully compact bathroom that is entered though a trompe l'oeil door. Little noise (this is a private-access cul-de-sac), and Hyde Park, the Albert Hall and Harrods all within a five-minute walk. A perfect place.

rooms	1 double.
price	£85-£90. Singles £65-£70.
meals	Continental breakfast included.
closed	Occasionally.
tube	Knightsbridge.
bus	9, 10, 14, 52. 74.

	Mary Williams
tel	07767 261667
fax	020 7581 0395
e-mail	bivvywilliams@hotmail.com

B&B

Map 1 Entry 65

Sterling Street
Knightsbridge, London SW7

These 1840 houses were built for the officers of the Household Cavalry, whose Knightsbridge barracks are close by. This particular house was once home to Bruce Bairnsfather, the WWI cartoonist, and you will find prints of his work in the house. You are plum in the heart of Knightsbridge here, a short stroll for the museums, Harrods, Hyde Park and the tube, and you get the whole of this smart open-plan basement to yourself. Incredibly, it is for people travelling on their own, and given that singles so often get a bad deal, it is good to see a little luxury put aside specifically for them. It is a great base, a big place, airily decorated in yellow, with an open fireplace, a good sofa, a couple of TVs and a Zulu shield on one wall. There is a small kitchen, and breakfast is bought down the night before and left in the fridge for you to help yourself whenever you wish. You also have your own entrance, making this a very private place. The bedroom is at the back of the house and overlooks a small garden, the bathroom is in the old coal cellar. A sensational single: safe, stylish and central.

rooms	1 single.
price	£72.
meals	Help-yourself continental breakfast included.
closed	Occasionally.
tube	Knightsbridge.
bus	9, 10, 14, 52, 74.

	Uptown Reservations
tel	020 7351 3445
fax	020 7351 9383
e-mail	inquiries@uptownres.co.uk

B&B

Map 1 Entry 66

37 Trevor Square
Knightsbridge, London SW7 1DY

A fabulous find, luxury in the middle of Knightsbridge. Trevor Square is incredibly pretty, unexpectedly peaceful and only a three-minute walk from Hyde Park or Harrods. Margaret runs an interior design company, rather successfully by the look of things. Impeccable furniture and furnishings throughout, including Nina Campbell *toile de Jouy*, wooden floors, stone busts and warm rugs in the dining room. In the large bedroom you'll find every mod con, a complimentary bar, an electric blanket, a cashmere duvet and maple tables. You get the top floor to yourself, including a hugely luxurious marbled bathroom (big mirrors, deep bath, power shower). There's a twin room, too. Margaret does breakfast down in the dining room (you get the full English works, or smoked salmon and scrambled eggs), and she'll light the fire in winter. There's a snug conservatory/sitting room you're welcome to use, too. You'll find hundreds of restaurants on your doorstep. And just in case you've forgotten, the Harrods' sales are in January and June.

rooms	2: 1 double, 1 twin sharing bath & shower (same-party bookings only).
price	£120. Singles £100.
meals	Full English breakfast included.
closed	Occasionally.
tube	Knightsbridge.
bus	9, 10, 14, 19, 22, 52, 74, 137.

	Margaret & Holly Palmer
tel	020 7823 8186
fax	020 7823 9801
e-mail	margaret@37trevorsquare.co.uk
web	www.37trevorsquare.co.uk

B&B

Map 1 Entry 67

Knightsbridge Green Hotel
159 Knightsbridge, London SW1X 7PD

This hotel has a battalion of faithful guests who return for the central location, the reasonable prices, the unfussy rooms and the ever-present Paul. He tries to greet everyone personally during their stay, and if you meet him by the lift, he'll chauffeur you up to your room. This is a family-owned hotel and you can expect to be greeted genuinely and warmly. Spotlessly clean bedrooms tend to be fairly simple, but they are surprisingly big, and while the design may be simple it is also pleasing, and you get a little sparkle. There are marble bathrooms, off-white walls, canvas curtains and air-conditioning. The hotel doesn't have a bar, but it is licensed and drinks are brought to your room, as is breakfast: croissants, freshly-squeezed orange juice, bacon and sausages from Harrods, if you want. Rooms at the back have been vibrantly decorated to make up for the lack of light in the stairwell and a couple of the rooms are nicely old-fashioned with warm floral fabrics and big beds (and especially popular with long-standing guests). All things Knightsbridge are on your doorstep, with the tube a hop and skip across the road.

rooms	28: 7 singles, 4 twins, 5 doubles, 12 suites.
price	£115-£145. Singles £90-£110 .Suites from £140-£170. Singles £90-£110.
meals	Breakfast £3.50-£10.50.
closed	Never.
tube	Knightsbridge.
bus	9, 10, 14, 19, 22, 52, 74, 137.

	Paul Fizia
tel	020 7584 6274
fax	020 7225 1635
e-mail	reservations@thekghotel.com
web	www.thekghotel.co.uk

Hotel

Map 1 Entry 68

16 William Mews
Knightsbridge, London SW1X 9HF

A cul-de-sac mews in the middle of Knightsbridge; it's so quiet you can hear birds sing. This is the epicentre of Knightsbridge; the Beatles once lived in the street, and if you fall out of bed, you land in Harvey Nicks. An easy house to find – it's the one with the flower pots outside: geraniums, camellias and lavender add a sweep of colour. You get the whole of the basement to yourself, the only drawback being pavement lights in the bedroom (you're unlikely to mind). It's only for the nimble, though: a narrow spiral staircase leads down. You'll find bedroom, sitting room, bathroom. There are Japanese prints and 1920s fashion posters on the walls, loads of guides, a tapestry hanging above the bed and a simple lived-in feel. There's a lovely yellow single on the first floor, with a faux-marble bathroom, mirrors, flowers, good art – very smart. Breakfast is taken at a table on which a mythical Greek beauty has been hand-painted. Around you Cuban art mixes with classical pictures. Pots and pans hang from the ceiling and gilt mirrors sparkle. Hyde Park is a two-minute walk, as are hundreds of restaurants.

rooms	2: 1 double (with sofa bed), 1 single.
price	£75–£85 (sofa bed £35). Singles £55–£65.
meals	Continental breakfast included.
closed	Occasionally.
tube	Knightsbridge.
bus	9, 10, 14, 19, 22, 52, 137.

	Mary Potter
tel	020 7259 6645
e-mail	marypotter@london01.fsnet.co.uk

B&B

Map 1 Entry 69

Basil Street Hotel

8 Basil Street, Knightsbridge, London SW3 1AH

The Basil does not follow fads and fashions, it is far too English for that. It is a throwback to the days of Empire, a place one might expect to find in India rather than in SW3. It is where diplomats gather for tea and where the Major-General holds the regimental dinner. The Gallery walkway is modelled on that of an old P&O liner, with writing desks in alcoves and a parliamentary clock upon the wall. At supper, dine on lobster bisque and roast rib of Scottish beef while the pianist plays gentle melodies from the past and the waiter asks, "will you have the bread and butter pudding, sir?". Run by eccentrics for eccentrics, this is the hotel that people who hate hotels adore. It is spread over six luxurious floors, though you should not expect to land on the first floor if you press '1' in the lift; that would be too easy. Bedrooms, which vary in size but not style, are liberally sprinkled with antiques, as is the rest of the hotel. You'll find Delft-tiled fireplaces, French armoires and Edwardian writing desks. Brilliant. *Weekend rates from £210 including breakfast*.

rooms	80: 21 doubles, 22 twins, 4 family, 33 singles.
price	£240. Family rooms £325. Singles £170.
meals	Breakfast £11-£15. Lunch & dinner £15-£30. Afternoon tea £12.50. Room service.
closed	Never.
tube	Knightsbridge.
bus	9, 10, 14, 19, 22, 52, 74, 137.

	Charles Lagares
tel	020 7581 3311
fax	020 7581 3693
e-mail	info@thebasil.com
web	www.thebasil.com

Hotel

Map 1 Entry 70

L'Hotel

28 Basil Street, Knightsbridge, London SW3 1AS

L'Hotel is well-named – it has the feel of a small Parisian hotel, but chief among its many bounties is Isabel, who, in her reign (long live the Queen), has proved it is not only what you do, but how you do it that matters. Her way is infectious; she is kind and open and nothing is too much trouble. The hotel's not bad either. Downstairs there's a great little restaurant/bar – the social hub of the place – where the odd note of jazz rings out and where wines come direct from the hotel's French vineyard. You can have breakfast down there (excellent coffee in big bowls, pains au chocolat and hot croissants from the hotel bakery), or up in your room, while you laze about on vast beds that are covered in Egyptian cotton, with Nina Campbell fabric on the walls, little box trees on the mantlepiece and original art on the walls. Turn left on your way out and Harvey Nicks is a hundred paces; turn right and Harrods is closer. If you want to eat somewhere fancy, try the Capital next door. It has a big reputation, is owned by the same family (the Levins), and Isabel will book you in. A very friendly, very pretty place.

rooms	12: 11 twins/doubles, 1 suite.
price	£200. Suite £215. Singles £175.
meals	Continental breakfast included, full English £6.50. Lunch & dinner £5-£20.
closed	Never.
tube	Knightsbridge.
bus	14, 19, 22, 52, 74, 137.

	Isabel Murphy
tel	020 7589 6286
fax	020 7823 7826
e-mail	reservations@lhotel.co.uk
web	www.lhotel.co.uk

Hotel

Map 1 Entry 71

Searcy's Roof Garden Bedrooms

30 Pavilion Road, Knightsbridge, London SW1X 0HJ

This is a real one-off, the sort of place you could only find in England. From the street you enter directly into a 1927 freight elevator (it's had a face-lift), then ascend three floors – by-passing Searcy's, the 160-year-old catering company whose headquarters these are. And step out of the lift to find extremely comfortable rooms (with extremely comfortable prices). These have been here since the mid-1960s, grand enough to ignore passing fashions, their sense of solid tradition almost aristocratic. Not that you should take this to be a euphemism for 'faded'. On the contrary, the rooms are delightful and fresh. Pretty fabrics and wallpaper give a county-house feel, there are canopied beds, lovely flowers, a smattering of antiques and smart new bathrooms (with the odd bath actually in the bedroom). Breakfast is brought to you, and accompanied occasionally by the sound of the Household Cavalry passing below. Exceptional value so close to Harrods, with Hyde Park and the Serpentine a short stoll. Marvellous.

rooms	10: 4 doubles, 3 twins, 2 singles, 1 suite.
price	£140. Suite £170. Singles £95-£120.
meals	Continental breakfast included.
closed	Christmas & New Year.
tube	Knightsbridge.
bus	9, 10, 14, 19, 22, 52, 74, 137.

Alexandra Saric
tel	020 7584 4921
fax	020 7823 8694
e-mail	rgr@searcys.co.uk
web	www.searcys.co.uk

Hotel

Map 1 Entry 72

57 Pont Street

Knightsbridge, London SW1X 0BD

A grand old London building – red-brick, high ceilings, ornate plaster work – brought into the 21st century with a funky makeover of pinks, browns, reds and whites. Number 57 is a minimalist's dream: space, clean lines, no clutter. In reception, there are high stools at a marbled bar, leather armchairs for the daily papers, the odd strip of shiny neon embedded in a wall and ivory-coloured silk curtains draped over a door. There is a lift to whisk you around, but if you take the stairs, you pass landings full of mirrored doors, busts on plinths and more draped silk. Contemporary bedrooms have neutral colours on the walls, cedar-wood blinds, big, suede armchairs, plasma-screen TVs and a piece or two of modern art. Some rooms are big, some are smaller, none are small. You get a bit of colour – a blue wall, a red carpet – and first-floor rooms have high ceilings; one has a balcony. There are woollen blankets, crisp white linen, and multi-jet showers in sparkling bathrooms. Back downstairs, cherry-red walls in a warm and stylish sitting room, with brown cord sofas and an open fire. Stylishly central.

rooms	20: 13 doubles, 4 twins, 2 singles, 1 suite.
price	£195–£265. Singles from £125. Suite £295. Weekend rates available.
meals	Continental breakfast £10. Room service.
closed	Never.
tube	Knightsbridge; Sloane Square.
bus	19, 22, 137.

	Nikki Kingdom
tel	020 7590 1090
fax	020 7590 1099
e-mail	no57@no57.com
web	www.no57.com

Hotel

Map 4 Entry 73

The Beaufort

33 Beaufort Gardens, Knightsbridge, London SW3 1PP

Two minutes from Harrods (they should hold an annual race, first one to get to the haberdashery), but even diehard shopaholics may linger just a little longer in their luxurious rooms. This was the first private-house hotel to open in London and it still has the feel of a home-from-home, albeit quite a grand one. A small reception, a complimentary bar, the morning papers in the sitting room and flowers everywhere. Porters swoop and carry bags upstairs to fabulous rooms. These vary in size and price, but some of the doubles are not much smaller than the suites, and if you imagine all the little (and big) extras you'd like to find in a room – well, they're here: fresh flowers, marble bathrooms, towelling bathrobes, bowls of fruit, the best linen, plush fabrics, CD players, air conditioning, modem points... if they haven't got it and you need it, they'll do their best to find it for you. Breakfast is brought to your room (starched linen tablecloths, Wedgwood china). A relaxing, spoiling place, with dedicated staff who give the place a very friendly feel, and it's in a cul-de-sac, so there's hardly any noise.

rooms	29: 18 twins/doubles, 7 suites, 4 singles.
price	£230–£305. Singles from £185. Suites from £325.
meals	Continental breakfast included. Room service available.
closed	Never.
tube	Knightsbridge.
bus	14, 74.

	Anna Bambrook
tel	020 7584 5252
fax	020 7589 2834
e-mail	reservations@thebeaufort.co.uk
web	www.thebeaufort.co.uk

Hotel

Map 4 Entry 74

Parkes Hotel

41 Beaufort Gardens, Knightsbridge, London SW3 1PW

A top-to-bottom refurbishment, an entire renovation, a cool three million lavished on this lap of luxury, and the result: perfection down to the tiniest detail. In the Italian-marble bathrooms you get heated floors and mirrors, shower heads the size of cymbals, deep cast-iron baths and mountains of towels. Bedrooms are no less indulging: huge rooms, high ceilings, sleigh beds, stunning fabrics, glistening chandeliers, modem points, DVD players, 18 different malts in the mini-bar. Nothing disappoints, least of all the service. There are rich Georgian colours on the walls – reds and yellows, greens and clarets – air conditioning in every room, sofas or armchairs, too. If you're thinking of opening a hotel and you'd like to see how it should be done, come here. Or, just relax in style. Harrods is a two-minute walk from this peaceful, tree-lined square. Stroll up to Hyde Park (and pass some of London's most expensive residential real estate on the way) or head for great local restaurants. Try San Lorenzo's (Princess Diana's favourite), Zuma for Japanese, or Toto's for great pasta.

rooms	32: 4 singles, 9 doubles, 2 twins, 17 suites.	
price	£280–£340. Suites £380–£490. Singles £230.	
meals	Full English breakfast £10–£15.	
closed	Never.	
tube	Knightsbridge.	
bus	14, 74.	

	Susan Burns
tel	020 7581 9944
fax	020 7581 1999
e-mail	info@parkeshotel.com
web	www.parkeshotel.com

Hotel

Map 4 Entry 75

Imperial College London
Watts Way, Princes Gardens, South Kensington, London SW7 1LU

Here's something outstanding. Two hundred paces from the Albert Hall, the campus accommodation of Imperial College London (five Nobel prizewinners) is open to all during the Easter and summer holidays. I saw Beit Hall, an exceptionally comfortable place, where rooms are big and bright, well-decorated, spotlessly clean, nothing to complain about (and many in the east wing have views of the Albert Hall). Extraordinarily, they keep the whole place running for you – cafés, bars, shops – though the sports centre is being rebuilt and won't reopen until 2006. There's a full cleaning service, linen and towels are all thrown in – I can't emphasise enough how nice the place is. Expect barbecues in the landscaped quad, subsidised beer, internet access, airport pick-ups, banks, shops, everything you'll need. You can stroll about, see the quads, the Queen's Tower, the College gardens. All the big museums are around the corner (Imperial owns the land, and private tours led by curators can be arranged for groups). Hyde Park is on your doorstep, and it's great for the Proms (August/September).

rooms	1,196: mix of twins and singles, some with showers, others sharing baths and showers.
price	£80–£85. Singles £42–£65.
meals	Breakfast included. Lunch & dinner from £5.
closed	Open during Easter & summer holidays only.
tube	South Kensington.
bus	9, 10, 14, 52, 74.

Marie Wilcox
tel	020 7594 9507
fax	020 7594 9504
e-mail	accommodationlink@imperial.ac.uk
web	www.imperial-accommodationlink.com

University Hall of Residence

Map 4 Entry 76

Aster House

3 Sumner Place, South Kensington, London SW7 3EE

The small water garden out back is something of a wildlife-magnet: ducks come to breed in spring, and a couple have made it their permanent residence. A very welcoming small hotel in South Kensington with an unexpectedly beautiful, first-floor conservatory where you breakfast on croissants and scrambled eggs while sitting under a vaulted-glass ceiling shielded from the sun by bamboo blinds. Not a place overflowing with antiques, but an extremely comfortable one none the less. Smart red carpets run throughout and bedrooms come with lots of trimmings: air conditioning, marble bathrooms and orthopaedic mattresses. You get cleverly stencilled walls (they look ancient), architectural prints, gilt-framed mirrors and a globe on the stairs. There are fresh flowers, pretty fabrics, halogen lighting and crowns above the beds. One room at the back has French windows that open onto the garden. A very elegant terrace at the front of the house has box hedging, plinths and urns, smart black railings and topiary. Lots of local restaurants: try the nearby Builder's Arms for stylish gastropub food.

rooms	14: 10 twins/doubles, 3 singles, 1 four-poster.
price	£160-£210. Singles £90-£115.
meals	Continental breakfast included.
closed	Never.
tube	South Kensington.
bus	14.

	Simon & Leonie Tan
tel	020 7581 5888
fax	020 7584 4925
e-mail	asterhouse@btinternet.com
web	www.asterhouse.com

Hotel

Map 4 Entry 77

Onslow Square
South Kensington, London SW3

Like all good London squares, this one has a fine supporting cast: Edwin Lutyens, the architect, was born at No 16, Thackeray wrote *The Virginians* at No 36, and Admiral Robert Fitzroy (who ferried Darwin to the Galapagos Islands) lived at No 38. Kay lives in a 1950s apartment block (this was a WWII direct hit), and in good weather you can breakfast on croissants and coffee on her small balcony while watching stylish South Kensington life pass by. The inside sparkles in white. Afternoon light pours in giving the place a bright and airy feel. There are ivory sofas, vases of lilies, parquet floors and walls of books. The bedroom is small, with a smart bed dressed in crisp white linen and a ceiling fan to cool in summer. You are free to use the place as home: make tea in the kitchen, read in the sitting room, or borrow the key to the communal gardens (the rarest of London treats), then hide away in blissful peace. The tube is a two-minute walk (direct to Heathrow), London's trendiest shops are on your doorstep and hundreds of restaurants wait; try Il Falconiere for popular family-cooked Italian.

rooms	1 double with separate shower.
price	£95. Singles £72.
meals	Continental breakfast included.
closed	Occasionally.
tube	South Kensington
bus	14, 49, 70, 74, 345.

	Uptown Reservations
tel	020 7351 3445
fax	020 7351 9383
e-mail	inquiries@uptownres.co.uk

B&B

Map 4 Entry 78

Sydney House Chelsea
9-11 Sydney Street, Chelsea, London SW3 6PU

Film-star good looks at Sydney House, but the beauty here runs deep, and unlike many 'cool' hotels, this one has a heart, setting it apart for the crowd. At the helm is Vojin – easy-going, humourous, utterly dedicated – and he, too, makes the place special. As for the seductive qualities of Sydney House, take your pick from... an open-plan bar where you can mix your own drinks; super-sleek in-built suede sofas; brightly polished American oak floors; and leather armchairs from the people who make the seats for Ferrari. Bedrooms upstairs are equally spoiling with halogen spots, hardwood floors, flat-screen TVs and Designers Guild chairs; a couple at the front have balconies. Wonderfully comfortable beds wear Sunday-best Frette linen and cashmere blankets, while smarter-than-smart bathrooms come with fluffy towels, waffle bathrobes, big mirrors and power showers. The Room at the Top is up in the eaves and has an enormous roof terrace. Breakfast on hot croissants, French butter and strong coffee, then head for that mecca of shopping, the King's Road – it's on your doorstep. Superb.

rooms	21: 8 doubles, 12 twins/doubles, 1 'Room at the Top'.
price	£175-£210. 'Room at the Top' £250.
meals	Continental breakfast included, full English £9.95. Room service.
closed	Christmas.
tube	South Kensington.
bus	11, 14, 19, 22, 49.

	Vojin Mandic
tel	020 7376 7711
fax	020 7376 4233
e-mail	info@sydneyhousechelsea.com
web	www.sydneyhousechelsea.com

Hotel

Map 4 Entry 79

4 First Street

Chelsea, London SW3 2LD

This is a smart London home in one of London's most desirable quarters. You get the top floor to yourself, and some floor it is. You're nicely private, it's surprisingly quiet, there's masses of space and the luxuries are unremitting. A sparkling bathroom of marble and mirrors has a deep bath in which to soak, while the bedroom is delightfully furnished with trim carpets, comfy armchairs, stencilled dressers and pretty pictures, and a wall of glass opens onto a tiny muralled balcony. Shirley won't thank me for saying it, but she's one of the nicest people you're likely to meet in London (I say this even though she works for a rival guide!). Her house is warmly welcoming, a perfect home-from-home. You breakfast in the basement by an open fire, you can catch the sun on the pretty decked terrace with pots and olive trees around you. Outside, there's lots to do. This is shop-till-you-drop land: Walton Street, South Kensington, Sloane Street and King's Road, are all on your doorstep. Stop for coffee at Baker & Spice (you can't get posher), and don't miss La Brasserie for supper. Fabulous.

rooms	1 double.
price	£105. Singles £75.
meals	Continental breakfast included.
closed	Occasionally.
tube	Sloane Square; Knightsbridge; South Kensington.
bus	14, 19, 22, 137.

	Shirley Eaton
tel	020 7581 8429
e-mail	shirley@eaton3176.fsnet.co.uk

B&B

Map 4 Entry 80

409 Nell Gwynn House

Sloane Avenue, Sloane Square, London SW3 3BB

This is a self-catering studio apartment in an Art Deco mansion block (the envy of all Europe when built in 1933). It is impeccable – central, stylish, very well-priced – a brilliant base for those in London for a week or two. It has recently been renovated in contemporary style. A small designer kitchen runs along one wall, and is fitted with everything you'll need (fridge, freezer, oven, microwave, dishwasher). There are light wood floors and big windows that look down on the smart streets of Chelsea (and you have a supermarket across the road). It's spacious, with a good red sofa, a stainless steel kitchen bar, and a step up to a comfy double bed. The whole place has been brilliantly thought out to maximise the space, giving it a warm, airy feel. You'll find blinds that soundproof, an LCD TV that swivels round so you can watch telly in bed and a hi-fi system that has speakers in the ceiling. The bathroom is exceptional in shiny white, and there's a washing machine tucked away in the built-in wardrobe. A real, not-to-be-missed, discovery – a little slice of luxury in SW3. Complete with concièrge.

rooms	1 studio double.
price	£450–£550 per week; £250–£350 for 3 nights.
meals	Self-catering; full kitchen facilities.
closed	Rarely.
tube	Sloane Square, South Kensington.
bus	14, 19, 22, 74, 137.

	Clare & Robin Dunipace
tel	01993 822171
fax	01993 824125
e-mail	clare.dunipace@amserve.net
web	www.oxford-cotswold-holidays.com

Self-Catering

Map 4 Entry 81

20 Bywater Street
Chelsea, London SW3 4XD

Another great find. Bywater Street is a cul-de-sac off the King's Road –
soundproofed, yet close to the shops. It's also one of those London streets where
residents paint their houses in marzipan colours, thus creating an architectural
rainbow. Incredibly, these were workmen's houses when built in 1857. Now they
are as desirable as any you'll find in London (John Le Carré let Smilie live here).
Richard and Caroline are extremely welcoming, give tea or coffee on arrival, then
pass on all the local secrets. The bedroom is downstairs, a pretty room, spotlessly
clean, with warm lighting, stripes and checks, a trim carpet and a wicker chair.
Expect fresh flowers, loads of mags and a CD player, too. The shower room is next
door (fluffy towels, coloured tiles), while breakfast is taken across the hall in the
kitchen/conservatory, a bright and cheery room that swims in morning sun.
Doors open onto a smallish paved garden full of terracotta pots. Sloane Square is a
five-minute walk, King's Road is at the top of the street. Try the Coopers Arms
for both good food and fine ale. An exceptional central London address.

rooms	1 double with separate shower.
price	£95-£100. Singles from £65.
meals	Continental breakfast included.
closed	Occasionally.
tube	Sloane Square.
bus	11, 19, 22, 137, 211.

	Caroline & Richard Heaton-Watson
tel	020 7581 2222
fax	020 7581 2222
e-mail	caheatonw@aol.com

B&B

Map 4 Entry 82

Chelsea Embankment
Chelsea, London SW3

Incredibly, this 1880 Norman Shaw building was originally one home. It is now a mansion block of seven apartments, this one having a slightly labyrinthine ramble to it. First and foremost, it is a family home, where two young boys roam politely. Secondly, it is a house of art, and there are walls of the stuff – books, paintings, sculptures, even a couple of Han dynasty figurines. You breakfast amid the splendour of Corinthian pillars in the duck-egg-blue dining room, with views across both road and river to a huge golden statue of Buddha in Battersea Park. There are stripped wood floors, a grand piano, an open fire, spectacular art. Pretty rooms are simple, yet smart – stylishly homely. The double is tucked away quietly at the back of the house. There are watercolours tumbling yellow curtains, crisp linen and Moroccan glass tooth mugs. The twin is slightly more contemporary, with directors chairs and a splash of colour. Emma makes homemade breads and jams, and there's garden honey from the Chelsea Physic Garden, where she works as a volunteer. The Viceroy of India, once lived next door.

rooms	2: 1 double, 1 twin (same-party bookings only).
price	£95. Singles £72.
meals	Continental breakfast included.
closed	Occasionally.
tube	Sloane Square (12-minute walk).
bus	137, 239.

Uptown Reservations
tel	020 7351 3445
fax	020 7351 9383
e-mail	inquiries@uptownres.co.uk

B&B

Map 4 Entry 83

Tite Street

Chelsea, London SW3

This 1890 apartment block was originally a theatre and Gloria's fourth-floor apartment was once home to the actress Elenor Glynn (as in the limerick). Gloria, herself an artist, recently appeared in a French movie, so she too has been immortalised. Wander around her home and come across Dutch milk urns, gold-leaf carvings, Regency dressing tables, Burmese boxes, potted busts, splashy oils, wonderful stuff. Not an eccentric home; rather an oasis of quiet English individuality – delightfully surprising and wholly authentic. The bedroom (sheets from Bloomingdales) is on the small side, but if you like the sound of the place you won't mind, and Gloria's next-door studio is yours to use as a sitting room. Better still is her large, lush roof garden for magical views across a landscape of London's rooftops and spires (perfect for Chelsea Flower Show one-upmanship). Breakfast (anytime after 8.30am) includes freshly squeezed juice (blood-red oranges), bread from the French bakery, exotic fruits and Columbian coffee. And there's Clover, the minature wire-haired daschund, too.

rooms	1 double.
price	£95. Singles £72.
meals	Continental breakfast included.
closed	Occasionally.
tube	Sloane Square (10-minute walk).
bus	11, 19, 22, 211, 319.

	Uptown Reservations
tel	020 7351 3445
fax	020 7351 9383
e-mail	inquiries@uptownres.co.uk

B&B

Map 4 Entry 84

Windermere Hotel
142-144 Warwick Way, Pimlico, London SW1V 4JE

This is a neat little family-run hotel where you get to meet the owners when you check in. Nick and Sylvia are Greek Cypriots and do things in the mediterranean-style; share the work, chat to guests, make the coffee. A smart exterior, floodlit at night, brims with colour courtesy of pretty window boxes. Inside, a simple décor favours yellow, though bedrooms are all different. Go for the slightly more expensive rooms at £130, which offer good value for money and have more than a dash of style. There are marble bathrooms, padded headboards, trim carpets and sweeping crowns above the beds. You get ceiling fans and TVs, fridges and armchairs. Early arrivals and departures are accommodated generously, and if you arrive fresh off the plane, you are likely to be met with the offer of breakfast. This is taken downstairs in the snug dining room, which transforms into a restaurant at night, delivering homemade dishes at reasonable prices (shepherd's pie for £8, Cajun chicken for £10, Smithfield steaks for £13). There's a small bar, too. Victoria is close, making this a pretty central spot run with much warmth.

rooms	22: 4 singles, 17 twins/doubles, 1 suite.
price	£104-£129. Singles £66-£99. Suite £145.
meals	Full English breakfast included. Dinner from £8. Limited room service.
closed	Never.
train	Victoria (Gatwick).
tube	Victoria; Sloane Square.
bus	11, 211, 239.

	Nick & Sylvia Hambi
tel	020 7834 5163
fax	020 7630 8831
e-mail	reservations@windermere-hotel.co.uk
web	www.windermere-hotel.co.uk

Hotel

Map 5 Entry 85

Denbigh Street
Pimlico, London SW1

Thomas Cubitt, who built Pimlico, has a statue at the end of the street and you may wish to go and thank him; the basement of this smart Victorian terraced house is pure heaven. You get it all to yourself – a suite of stylish rooms with a tiny courtyard garden and your own private entrance. There are plantation shutters at the front, a waterfall of pillows on the bed, leather bedside tables and double doors that open onto a small sitting room. The style is warmly contemporary, with airy high-ceilinged rooms, halogen spotlights and light wood floors. Minimalist elegance in the bedroom comes courtsey of a suede headstead, crisp linen bedclothes and pure wollen blankets. Through in the sitting room there's a good sofa, a TV and CD player, and a huge gilt mirror above the fire place. The room stretches through a small kitchen to doors that open onto the garden (spot-lit at night). Breakfast is left in the fridge, a help-yourself affair that leads to lazy mornings, but you'll get out of bed for the sparkling bathroom: an enormous glass shower, a deep cast-iron bath, fluffy white towels, the lap of luxury.

rooms	1 double.
price	£95. Singles £72.
meals	Help-yourself continental breakfast included.
closed	Occasionally.
train	Victoria (to Gatwick).
tube	Pimlico; Victoria.
bus	2, 24, 36, 88.

	Uptown Reservations
tel	020 7351 3445
fax	020 7351 9383
e-mail	inquiries@uptownres.co.uk

B&B

Map 5 Entry 86

Tachbrook Street
Pimlico, London SW1

Claire and John deal in historical ephemera and their home overflows. There are old menus, cards and photographs, even an illuminated document that dates to 1560. There is always something to catch the eye, be it a five-foot-high candlestick in the colourful basement dining room or an exceptional post-Stalinist oil painting in the grand first-floor sitting room. Most wonderful of all is the spectacular hand-painted cornicing and ceiling roses; delicate greens, reds and golds float across the ceiling. In one bedroom, a Christmas cactus and Borneo pheasant feathers on top of a mahogany wardrobe, greenery spilling out of brass pots on plinths, original pine shutters, a Cubitt fireplace and a couple of 1938 mahogany beds. The second bedroom is bigger, less cluttered, but wonderfully pleasing, with carafes of water, a huge Dyak hat from Brunei and a Victorian medicine chest that holds a bottle of Dr Gregory's Stomach Powder. Bathrooms are separate, but Egyptian robes get you to them in style. Claire and John own a nearby shop, so pop in for a look. A delightfully eccentric English home.

rooms	2: 1 double, 1 twin, both with separate bath.
price	£95. Singles £72.
meals	Continental breakfast included.
closed	Occasionally.
train	Victoria (to Gatwick).
tube	Pimlico; Victoria.
bus	2, 24, 36, 88.

	Uptown Reservations
tel	020 7351 3445
fax	020 7351 9383
e-mail	inquiries@uptownres.co.uk

The Sloane Hotel

29 Draycott Place, Sloane Square, London SW3 2SH

A treasure-trove hotel, one of the loveliest in this book. Everywhere you look something magical catches the eye, be it a faux leopard-skin sofa, a gilded marble fireplace, or an ancient admiral's uniform looming in a corner. Xavier and Delphine came over from France and have infused the place with Gallic flair while keeping the traditions of an English hotel very much alive (afternoon tea when you return from Harvey Nicks, cocktails before you head off to Caraffini's). Heavenly bedrooms are out of this world: highlights include crushed velvet curtains on handmade four-posters, ragged paint on panelled walls, even a 25-foot-high draped bedhead. Rooms are stuffed with exquisite antiques, perhaps 1860 bedside lights, a 19th-century chestnut dresser, or a muralled mantelpiece mirror. There are quilted blankets, *Lelièvre* wallpaper, *toile de Jouy* fabrics, amazing oils, porcelain pots, armchairs and sofas dressed in the finest materials; the place is an A-Z of designers old and new. Exceptional service and attention to detail, a roof-top terrace, and the King's Road 50 yards from the front door. Spectacular.

rooms	22: 16 doubles, 6 suites.
price	£225–£270. Suites from £305. Singles £175.
meals	Full English breakfast £9–£12. Room service.
closed	Never.
tube	Sloane Square.
bus	11, 19, 22, 137, 211.

	Xavier & Delphine Colin
tel	020 7581 5757
fax	020 7584 1348
e-mail	reservations@sloanehotel.com
web	www.sloanehotel.com

Hotel

Map 4 Entry 88

The Draycott

26 Cadogan Gardens, Sloane Square, London SW3 2RP

A very indulging place – it's as if they've conspired to pamper you rotten. You get champagne on the house at six, and if you roll back in the early hours, you may get a night cap from Ali, the night manager. The Draycott is English to its core, a countryhouse in SW3, with an honesty bar in the drawing room and steps down to a communal garden where cherry trees blossom in spring. There are plush furnishings, the morning papers, old oils on the walls, even a post box at reception. Bedrooms are just as sumptuous, some huge, some big, with king-size beds and open-plan sitting areas. There are ancient wardrobes, mahogany tables, pretty writing desks, original prints. You find handwritten welcome notes on arrival, marble bathrooms, loads of storage space and tumbling curtains. Breakfast is brought to your room and properly set at the table. There's a daily maid service and room service, too; ring the chef and he'll try to come up with whatever you want. Sloane Street, the King's Road and the tube are all a two-minute stroll, and Tiffany's the jeweller's has opened up around the corner, so beware.

rooms	35: 6 singles, 18 doubles, 11 suites.
price	£260–£300. Suites from £440. Singles £140.
meals	Breakfast £14.50–£18.50.
closed	Never.
tube	Sloane Square.
bus	19, 22, 137.

	John Hanna
tel	020 7730 6466
fax	020 7730 0236
e-mail	reservations@draycotthotel.com
web	www.draycotthotel.co.uk

Hotel

Map 4 Entry 89

The London Outpost of Bovey Castle

69 Cadogan Gardens, Sloane Square, London SW3 2RB

This little enclave around Sloane Square is full of spoiling hotels, with none more spoiling than the Outpost, a perfect place to come in search of peace and privacy. An impeccable country-house style runs effortlessly throughout, with Irish linen, hot-water bottles, tartan blankets, and beds that are turned down each evening. The four-poster is so big it had to be built in its room, there are crystal glasses and decanters in the bedrooms, elegant sofas at the end of beds and seven rooms have open fires. Also: beautiful antique wardrobes and dressers, fresh flowers, oils, Scottish prints, marble plinths, sculpted busts, bowls of fruit – nothing but the best. Bags are carried up to rooms and newspapers come with breakfast (which you can have in your room or downstairs in the conservatory). Rooms are large, some are huge, and those at the top of the house have chimney-pots views. There's an honesty bar and each evening guests gather for a glass of champagne in the drawing room; it's on the house. You can even play croquet in the gardens across the road. Luxurious country-house living in the middle of the city.

rooms	11: 5 twins/doubles, 2 doubles, 3 suites, 1 four-poster.
price	£190-£270. Suites £320.
meals	Full English breakfast £11.95-£16.95. Room service.
closed	Christmas.
tube	Sloane Square.
bus	11, 19, 22, 137, 211.

	Caroline Nolan
tel	020 7589 7333
fax	020 7581 4958
e-mail	info@londonoutpost.co.uk
web	www.londonoutpost.co.uk

Hotel

Map 4 Entry 90

Clabon Mews

Sloane Square, London SW1

Here's something different. Not for Julie the reverence of English tradition. Instead, a 1980s mews house where you can hoover the (woollen-fabric) walls and where Kazakh hammocks hang from the ceiling. Julie, an artist (ex-bunny girl and airbrush operator) is cheerful and easy-going. She designed her house, then had it built from scratch. Don't expect the ordinary: big padded-leather chairs at a marble breakfast table, brick walls, a stainless steel spiral staircase (there's a lift, too) and a leather elephant. The first floor is one large sitting room, with a wall of glass at one end, thus light and airy. Julie is a big traveller and bits and bobs from around the world (hubble-bubble pipes, brass pots, a Syrian backgammon board) fill the room. The bedroom up on the second floor is trading in its woollen walls for painted ones. It is pretty (cane bed, lovely curtains, American oak doors, lots of storage) and very quiet; this is a small mews with nearly no traffic. You are free to go online, watch TV, sit in the courtyard garden. Knightsbridge, Chelsea, Sloane Square and South Kensington are on your doorstep.

rooms	1 double.
price	£95. Singles £72.
meals	Continental breakfast included.
closed	Occasionally.
tube	Sloane Square.
bus	19, 22, 137.

	Uptown Reservations
tel	020 7351 3445
fax	020 7351 9383
e-mail	inquiries@uptownres.co.uk

B&B

Map 4 Entry 91

Durley House

115 Sloane Street, Sloane Square, London SW1X 9PJ

Nothing but the best at Durley House, a grand home-from-home, where huge rooms are extravagantly furnished in English country-house style. This is a suite-only hotel, where service, style and space come in abundance. There are antique dressers, old chests, massive sofas and four-poster beds. Oils hang on the walls, chandeliers glisten. The Durley suite comes with an exquisitely carved overmantle and three floor-to-ceiling Georgian windows that open onto a balcony. Less expensive suites are equally impressive, with four-posters or half-tester beds, marble bathrooms and decanters of port in the sitting rooms. Breakfast arrives via a dumb waiter, while room service comes from butlers who set up tables in your sitting room. Each suite also has a fully-equipped kitchen, so you can cook for yourself; staff will even do your shopping. Just about anything can be arranged: fashion shows and private drinks parties are held in guest's rooms, chefs are brought in to cook. Expect all the extras (flowers, bathrobes, Roberts radios, twice-daily maid service) and tennis in the garden.

rooms	11: 8 1-bedroom suites, 3 2-bedroom suites.
price	1-bedroom suite £375–£495; 2-bedroom suites £565–£645; Durley suite £725.
meals	Breakfast £12.50–£18.50. 24-hour room service.
closed	Never.
tube	Sloane Square
bus	19, 22, 137.

	Stella Amor
tel	020 7235 5537
fax	020 7259 6977
e-mail	info@durleyhouse.com
web	www.durleyhouse.com

Hotel

Map 4 Entry 92

The Cadogan

75 Sloane Street, Knightsbridge, London SW1X 9SG

Oscar Wilde was arrested in Room 118, while Lillie Langtry sold her house to the hotel and you now dine in her drawing room. The Cadogan has been around since 1888 and the grand old lady of Sloane Street is smiling brightly these days; rejuvenated by a recent face-lift. Smoky purple walls and pink velvet chairs in the dining room, oak panelling and ornate cornicing in the drawing room and stained-glass windows and ostrich leather armchairs in the bar. There are chandeliers and ceiling roses, marble floors and the original elevator. Bedrooms come in two styles. Contemporary rooms are rich with fancy French fabrics, red leather headboards, silk curtains, high ceilings and flat-screen TVs. Head up a couple of floors and you come to the country-house rooms: William Morris fabrics, ornate fireplaces, crisp sheets and duvets, soothing yellows and greens. Suites are larger, have sofas, a couple of sparkling bathrooms and plates of exotic fruit. The gardens of Cadogan Place are just across the road and you are free to walk, sit, dream; tennis courts, too. The Number 19 bus stops outside the front door.

rooms	65: 7 singles, 40 twins/doubles, 18 suites.
price	£285-£355. Singles £190. Suites from £410.
meals	Breakfast £12-£16.50. Lunch & dinner £15-£35.
closed	Never.
tube	Sloane Square; Knightsbridge.
bus	19, 22, 137.

	Oliver Sevestre
tel	020 7235 7141
fax	020 7245 0994
e-mail	info@cadogan.com
web	www.cadogan.com

Hotel

Map 4 Entry 93

The Goring

Beeston Place, London SW1W 0JW

The Goring is a London institution, an epitome of Englishness, with a dining room for Dover sole or pheasant and a bar for oysters and champagne. Ninety-two years a hotel with a Goring ever at the helm, it is the oldest family-run hotel in London, built in 1910 by O R Goring, the first hotel in the world to have central heating and a private bathroom in every room. It is a grand place with its own traditions: George still holds a cocktail party for guests on Sunday evenings. Enter a world of marble floors, yellow walls and glittering chandeliers by the dozen. Liveried doormen at reception dress like Napoleonic generals (their manner more convivial, no doubt); one of them, Peter, has worked here for over 30 years. Good-sized bedrooms are as you'd expect – smart and traditional with a dash of flair: crisp linen, woollen blankets, plush carpets and fresh flowers. Rooms at the back have garden views. Huge attention to detail throughout the hotel and impeccable service from a devoted staff. Two minutes from Buckingham Palace, yet Beeston Place is remarkably quiet for central London. *Weekend rates available.*

rooms	74: 47 twins/doubles, 20 singles, 7 suites.
price	£300-£400. Suites from £400. Singles £235.
meals	Full English breakfast £12.50-£17.50. Lunch £25. Dinner £40. Room service.
closed	Never.
train	Victoria (to Gatwick).
tube	Victoria.
bus	2, 8, 16, 36, 38, 52, 73, 82.

	George Goring
tel	020 7396 9000
fax	020 7834 4393
e-mail	reception@goringhotel.co.uk
web	www.goringhotel.co.uk

Hotel

Map 5 Entry 94

22 Jermyn Street
St James's, London SW1Y 6HL

Stick a pin into the middle of a map of London and it will land in Jermyn Street. Built in 1680, and once home to luminaries such as Gladstone, Newton and Thackery, it is now best known for the bespoke shirt makers, who have made the street their own. Fittingly for one of London's smartest streets, it brings you one of London's smartest hotels. Number 22 is a perfect London base that does nothing but spoil you: roses in marble bathrooms, sofas to sink into, regal fabrics, crisp white linen, dramatic flowers erupting from glass vases. There are antique tables and writing desks, bowls of tangerines and walnuts. Cushions are plumped up by the chambermaids to a prescribed level, then the housekeeper comes in with her ruler to check! Staff are impeccable, kind and courteous; nothing is too much trouble. Go out at night for supper (try Rowley's across the road) and return to find your bed turned down; wake up in the morning and your breakfast will be brought to your room. Five minutes by foot from the front door and you find galleries, royal palaces, West End theatres, parks... and Fortnum & Mason for tea.

rooms	18: 5 doubles, 13 suites.
price	£245. Suites £345-£410.
meals	Continental breakfast £12.50. Room service.
closed	Never.
tube	Piccadilly Circus.
bus	9, 14, 19, 22, 38.

	Laurie Smith
tel	020 7734 2353
fax	020 7734 0750
e-mail	office@22jermyn.com
web	www.22jermyn.com

Hotel

Map 2 Entry 95

South Audley Street

Mayfair, Mayfair, London W1

This 1730 Mayfair house is a *bona fide* jaw-dropper – English to its core, effortlessly stylish, sumptuously elegant. There's a marble hall full of old oils and gilt mirrors, a first-floor sitting room with pretty garden views and a basement dining room where you'll breakfast with candelabra on the table, but it is the bedroom (up on the fourth floor, so no need to visit the health club) that will astound you. Expect the very best: ancient antiques, a French bamboo dresser, a huge mahogany wardrobe, smartly-dressed armchairs. The bed is gigantic, the art is delightful, and bay trees stand guard beyond Georgian windows. The room is huge, the style is clipped perfection – beyond reproach. It interlinks with a pretty single decorated in Indian *toile* fabrics, and has a sparkling bathroom. There is a further twin two flights up that's not quite as grand, but which is delightful nonetheless. Old London streets encircle you. Don't miss Pichoux for afternoon tea, the Mount Street Gardens, Grosvenor Chapel, the restaurants of Shepherd's Market or The Ritz. Fantastic B&B in the heart of old London. Hyde Park is close.

rooms	3: 1 double, 1 single sharing bath & shower (same party-bookings only); 1 twin with separate bath & shower.
price	£95. Singles £72.
meals	Continental breakfast included.
closed	Occasionally.
tube	Green Park.
bus	2, 8, 10, 16, 36, 73, 74, 82, 137.

	Uptown Reservations
tel	020 7351 3445
fax	020 7351 9383
e-mail	inquiries@uptownres.co.uk

B&B

Map 2 Entry 96

The Dorchester

Park Lane, Mayfair, London W1A 2HJ

Enter through revolving doors and be greeted by a battalion of liveried doormen, gliding effortlessly across marble floors under a gilded ceiling that defies overstatement. Keep going and you're in The Promenade, a stunningly beautiful room through which all Dorchester life flows. It is *the* place to linger – a window back in time to an England that once was – so come for afternoon tea or to sip champagne while the pianist plays. Bedrooms are what you'd expect: the crispest linen, the plushest fabrics, fabulous marble bathrooms, pure heaven. The Oliver Messel suite is considered one of the finest hotel suites in the world (and comes with a price tag of £2,500 a night), but all rooms elate. Downstairs in the piano bar there's Liberace's mirrored piano, while in the Grill Room you can eat the best roast beef in the world. You also get spas, saunas and steam rooms, hi-tech gadgetry coming out of your ears, and a private dining room where you can watch the cooks at work. I've hardly scratched the surface, but if you're looking for the show-stopping best, then this is it. *Weekend rates from £315, full breakfast included.*

rooms	250: 170 doubles, 30 twins, 50 suites.
price	£395-£510. Suites from £650. Singles from £325.
meals	Breakfast £19.50-£23. Lunch & dinner from £30. Room service.
closed	Never.
train	Victoria (to Gatwick).
tube	Hyde Park Corner; Green Park.
bus	2, 10, 16, 36, 73, 74, 82, 137.

	David Wilkinson
tel	020 7629 8888
fax	020 7409 0114
e-mail	reservations@dorchesterhotel.com
web	www.dorchesterhotel.com

Hotel

Map 1 Entry 97

Culross Street
Mayfair, London W1

Another extraordinary find, this one tucked away between Grosvenor Square and Hyde Park. Oxford Street is a two-minute stoll, New Bond Street a five-minute hike. The house was built during WWII, though you'd think it much older, and once inside you find a home that's happy to linger in an elegant past. June likes having guests and formalities are dropped. You're welcome to use her enormous sitting room, where she operates an honesty bar: help yourself to a whisky, then flop into one of her gargantuan sofas and gaze upon her beautiful art. The upstairs bedroom is more of a suite; the room is very large and has room for a sofa and armchair. In no particular order you get: jugs of water, a small bottle of sloe gin, an enormous mirror running above the beds, library steps for bedside tables, a TV and video and a military chest that turns into a desk. Expect a bust of Juno, gilt-framed pictures and a shoe horn in the huge marble bathroom. You breakfast in a muralled dining room at an old oak table sitting on Chippendale chairs. There's a delightful garden, too – big and shady, perfect for a summer doze.

rooms	1 twin.
price	£95. Singles £72.
meals	Continental breakfast included.
closed	Occasionally.
tube	Bond Street; Marble Arch.
bus	2, 10, 16, 36, 73, 74, 82, 137.

	Uptown Reservations
tel	020 7351 3445
fax	020 7351 9383
e-mail	inquiries@uptownres.co.uk

B&B

Map 1 Entry 98

22 York Street
Marylebone, London W1U 6PX

The Callis family live in two Regency townhouses in W1 – not your average London residence and one that defies all attempts to pigeonhole it. There may be 18 bedrooms, but you should still expect the feel of home: Michael is determined to keep things friendly and easy-going. This might explain the salsa dancing lessons that once broke out at breakfast, a meal of great conviviality taken communally around a curved wooden table in the big and bright kitchen/dining room. Here, a weeping ficus tree stands next to the piano, which, of course, you are welcome to play. There's always something to catch your eye, be it the red-lipped oil painting outside the dining room or the old boots on the landing. Wooden floors run throughout, and each house has a huge sitting room, one with a grand piano, the other with sofas, books and backgammon. Expect silk eiderdowns, good beds and lots of space in the bedrooms: all are spotless and very comfortable. This is Sherlock Holmes country and Madame Tussauds, Regent's Park and Lord's are all close by, as are hundreds of restaurants. A very friendly place.

rooms	18: A mix of twins, doubles, family & single rooms; 15 with bath, 3 with separate bath.
price	£100. Family rooms £141. Singles £82.25. Under 5s free.
meals	Continental breakfast included.
closed	Never.
train	Marylebone.
tube	Baker Street.
bus	2, 13, 30, 74, 82, 113, 139, 274.

	Michael & Liz Callis
tel	020 7224 2990
fax	020 7224 1990
e-mail	mc@22yorkstreet.co.uk
web	www.22yorkstreet.co.uk

B&B

Map 1 Entry 99

Number Ten

10 Manchester Street, Marylebone, London W1U 4DG

Number Ten offers a good night's sleep in the middle of town at very attractive prices. At weekends you can stay for as little as £100 a night (two-night minimum), a hugely popular deal, so book ahead. Rooms are simple and spotless, with good use of space and natural colours, comfortable beds and crisp linen. You get padded headboards, wicker chairs, TVs, hi-fis, fans and good bathrooms. Some rooms are bigger than others, but even the single rooms have space for a double bed, so don't expect a broom cupboard. This smart 1919 red-brick building was once a nurses' residence for the Middlesex hospital and elderly ladies occasionally turn up on nostalgic whims. Inside, there's a smart colonial feel to the sitting room (seagrass matting, bamboo blinds and big sofas), and a basement dining room for good buffet breakfasts (loads of fruit, rolls and pastries, freshly squeezed juice, coffee and tea). There's a lift and a 24-hour porter service; theatre tickets can be booked, taxis called. The Wallace Collection, which has reopened after years of magnificent restoration, is at the end of the road – unmissable.

rooms	46: 5 singles, 13 doubles, 19 twins, 9 suites.
price	£150. Suites £195. Singles £120.
meals	Continental breakfast included, full English £5.
closed	Never.
tube	Bond Street; Baker Street.
bus	2, 10, 23, 94, 137.

	Neville Isaac
tel	020 7486 6669
fax	020 7224 0348
e-mail	stay@10manchesterstreet.fsnet.co.uk
web	www.10manchesterstreet.com

Hotel

Map 1 Entry 100

23 Greengarden House

St Christopher's Place, Bond Street, London W1U 1NL

An enchanting pedestrianised street, so well hidden from the rest of London that some mapmakers don't know it exists. Window boxes burst with colour, pretty shops are hard to resist and the peace here at night is incredible for a city. Nikki runs a smooth ship at Greengarden House, making this a very friendly and hugely comfortable place to stay. These are smart, private, serviced apartments. Seventeen come in contemporary style (glass tables, neutral colours, Italian furniture, airy rooms), while six are more traditionally furnished (plush fabrics, antique dressers, padded headboards, bolder colours). All are lovely, the idea being to provide both style and substance, a gorgeous home-from-home in the centre of town. Thus, you get electronic wizardry in the sitting room, a hi-tech kitchen, an overdose of luxury in the bathroom, and a weekday maid service to keep it all clean. If you need something done, Nikki will see to it; nothing is too much trouble. A thriving restaurant district is on your doorstep (don't miss Pizza Paradiso) as are Mayfair, Bond Street and Marble Arch.

rooms	23: 15 1-bedroom apartments; 8 2-bedroom apartments.
price	1-bedroom apartments £230–£270; 2-bedroom apartments £320–£375.
meals	Full kitchen facilities.
closed	Never.
tube	Bond Street.
bus	2, 10, 12, 74, 137, 159.

	Nikki Pybus
tel	020 7935 9191
fax	020 7935 8858
e-mail	info@greengardenhouse.com
web	www.greengardenhouse.com

Serviced accomodation

Map 2 Entry 101

Five Maddox Street

Mayfair, London W1S 2QD

This is the epitome of London cool, a super-sleek, highly discreet central London wonderland. You find clean lines and effortless style everywhere. Terrazzo stone stairs sweep you up from the front door, polished plaster walls are sealed with beeswax. In reception, a wall of glass behind which tropical fish laze; in the suites, leather cushions on which to lounge in front of a fire. Expect pressed bamboo floors, linen kimonos, oil-burners in every room. There are glass tables, chenille sofas, creamy leather headboards, lacquered walls. Beds are dressed in crisp Egyptian cotton and faux-fur blankets, limestone bathrooms delight. Every room is a suite; two have gardens, several have balconies and the loft suite has a leather staircase. Every conceivable electronic gadget, including DVDs, fax machines, private lines... think of it, and you'll find it here. Four different types of breakfast (including 'Vitality' for hangovers), great room service from local restaurants, a kitchen stuffed with goodies from tomato soup to champagne, and chefs who come in to cook for you. Sotheby's and Soho are on your doorstep.

rooms	12: 9 1-bedroom suites, 2 2-bedroom suites, 1 3-bedroom suite.
price	1-bedroom suites £285-£405; 2-bedroom suites £525; 3-bedroom suite £705.
meals	Breakfast £8-£18. Room service.
closed	Never.
tube	Oxford Circus.
bus	3, 6, 8, 12, 15, 23, 88, 159.

	Tracy Lowy
tel	020 7647 0200
fax	020 7647 0300
e-mail	no5maddoxst@living-rooms.co.uk
web	www.no5maddoxst.com

Hotel

Map 2 Entry 102

West Street Hotel

13-15 West Street, Covent Garden, London WC2H 9HE

Turn left out of the front door and you land in Soho, turn right and you wash up in Covent Garden. Like its setting, West Street embodies the essence of London cool, and those in search of a bit of rock-star glamour will be in heaven. Incredible rooms indulge your every whim. 'Loft' takes up the whole of the top floor and comes with a high curved ceiling, orange tulip chairs, a fake cowhide rug and a fireplace where flames emerge though pebbles (very zen). One wall is glass, another is green slate, faux-fur blankets cover a massive bed and there's a sunken bath in a predictably huge bathroom. When guests are not staying, the room is used for fashion shoots and celebrity interviews. Two rooms share the floor below, one having a gigantic decked roof terrace and a bed with a creamy leather bedhead... nothing here is less than extraordinary. The odd bit of modern art hangs on the walls and bathroom smellies come courtesy of Kiehl's. Step in off the street and you enter EastatWest, a fusion restaurant and bar with golden lighting, red leather sofas and the odd statue of Buddha. DJs play at the weekends.

rooms	3 doubles.
price	£295; £410; £525.
meals	Full English breakfast included.
closed	Occasionally.
tube	Leicester Square; Covent Garden.
bus	14, 19, 24, 29, 38, 176.

	Tony Geary
tel	020 7010 8700
fax	020 7010 8601
e-mail	east.west@egami.co.uk
web	www.egami.co.uk

Hotel

Map 2 Entry 103

Hazlitt's
6 Frith Street, Soho, London W1D 5JA

One of the bathrooms has a safe hidden behind an oil painting, while in the sitting room, authors who stay leave signed copies of their books; it has become a tradition and the cabinet bulges. This is a wonderful hotel, a real London townhouse, terribly smart, delightfully cosy, a great place to stay in the heart of Soho. The house dates to 1718 and famous essayist William Hazlitt died here in 1830. Bedrooms are magnificent, not big, but what they lack in size they make up for in style. Expect antique desks, Georgian colours, claw-foot baths and carved wooden bedheads. There are gilt mirrors, silk curtains, oils on the walls and crushed velvet throws. Beds are smartly dressed in crisp linen, the odd floor slopes wildly and many rooms have ornate marble fireplaces. Breakfast is usually brought to your room, but guests sometimes head for Soho's famous cafés instead. Choose from Bar Italia (Latin-trendy), Maison Bertaux (bohemian, dates to 1871) or Patisserie Valerie (nicely Gallic). Mozart lived at Number 18 in 1765, and John Logie Baird first demonstrated his television at Number 22.

rooms	23: 19 doubles, 3 singles, 1 suite.
price	£240–£300. Singles £205. Suite £350.
meals	Continental breakfast £9.75.
closed	Never.
tube	Tottenham Court Road; Leicester Square.
bus	7, 8, 10, 14, 19, 24, 98, 159.

	Andy Boardman
tel	020 7434 1771
fax	020 7439 1524
e-mail	reservations@hazlitts.co.uk
web	www.hazlittshotel.co.uk

Hotel

Map 2 Entry 104

Manette Street
Soho, London W1

B&B in the heart of Soho; if you go to the theatre, you can pop home for drinks at half time. In *A Tale of Two Cities*, Dickens housed Dr Manette in the street, hence the name. At five in the afternoon, come home and sit out on Dennis's lovely terrace with a glass of wine while the bells of St Giles in the Fields peel. This is a 1950s apartment block on a surprisingly peaceful street, bang in the centre of town. 'Everything is just around the corner' with Trafalgar Square a five-minute stroll and Foyles bookshop at the end of the road. The apartment, over one floor, is on the small side, but there is much beauty within: fine art, old books, parquet floors, a Venetian glass fruit bowl. You breakfast in the sitting room / dining room (Betty, the housekeeper, makes the marmalade), and sleep under a small chandelier. There are padded bedheads, trim carpets, John Lewis linen and a TV. The bathroom next door is wonderfully old-fashioned and comes in lemon yellow. Make the most of Soho and all its haunts: Trattoria da Aldo (where the locals eat), Ronnie Scotts for jazz, the French House pub. Fantastic.

rooms	1 double.
price	£95. Singles £72.
meals	Continental breakfast included.
closed	Occasionally.
tube	Tottenham Court Road; Leicester Square.
bus	10, 14, 19, 24, 29, 38.

	Uptown Reservations
tel	020 7351 3445
fax	020 7351 9383
e-mail	inquiries@uptownres.co.uk

B&B

Map 2 Entry 105

University College London

Campbell House, 5-10 Taviton Street, Russell Square, London WC1H 0BX

A pioneering seat of learning, 'the Godless institution of Gower Street' was founded by 'an association of liberals' who took as their model the universities of Germany and Scotland and not the Church of England universities of Oxford and Cambridge. Thus, in 1828, education was made available to men regardless of their religion, and in 1878, to women. Fittingly, these halls of residence were once the home of Hugh Price Hughes, the Methodist preacher, who used to speak from one of the balconies. In summer you can stay for next to nothing. Rooms are basic: clean and tidy, with single beds, easy chairs, wardrobes and chests of drawers, and each corridor has a shared shower block. If you are looking for something cheap and cheerful close to the centre of town, you'll be hard pressed to find better. Breakfast is not included, but there are kitchens where you can store and prepare food, or you can eat out. Finally, the 'auto-iconic' body of the philosopher Jeremy Bentham remains in the university's South Cloister – they used to bring him out for certain suppers! Ask nicely and they may let you see him.

rooms	100: 40 twins, 60 singles; shower blocks shared on each corridor.
price	£40-£43. Singles £21-£23.
meals	Kitchens available for self-catering.
closed	Open mid-June to mid-September only.
train	Euston.
tube	Euston.
bus	59, 68, 91, 168.

	Residence Manager
tel	020 7679 1479
fax	020 7388 0060
e-mail	accommodation@ucl.ac.uk
web	www.ucl.ac.uk/residences

University Hall of Residence

Map 2 Entry 106

The Jenkins Hotel

45 Cartwright Gardens, Russell Square, London WC1H 9EH

David Suchet (aka Hercule Poirot) once stood under the pillared porch of the Jenkins Hotel, and even though the director got his shot, Hercule and his mischievous moustache didn't check in, thus calling into question the power of his little grey cells. Sam's quirky B&B hotel is extraordinary given both its price tag and the gentleness of its staff – this is more the sort of family operation you'd expect to find in France. No lift and five floors (no need for a fitness room, then) but a cantilevered staircase and the odd sloping floor instead. Bedrooms are spotless and have neat carpets, bright fabrics, padded headboards, sheets and blankets. Most rooms have the equivalent of a ship's shower; compact, but does the job nicely. You'll find the odd antique, mini bars, even safes, but each room is very different (in size as well as style), so if you have a particular requirement, ask when booking. Don't miss the fabulous North Sea Fish Restaurant in nearby Leigh Street for some of the best fish and chips in the capital. Regent's Park is close, and the British Library a short stroll. No smokers, please.

rooms	13: 8 twins/doubles, 5 family, 2 singles; 1 single, separate shower.
price	£85-£90. Singles £52-£72.
meals	Full English breakfast included.
closed	Never.
train	King's Cross; Euston.
tube	Russell Square; King's Cross; Euston.
bus	59, 68, 91, 168.

	Sam Bellingham
tel	020 7387 2067
fax	020 7383 3139
e-mail	reservations@jenkinshotel.demon.co.uk
web	www.jenkinshotel.demon.co.uk

Hotel

Map 2 Entry 107

Harlingford Hotel

61-63 Cartwright Gardens, Russell Square, London WC1H 9EL

The smart Georgian exterior of this hotel is picture-book pretty, with wandering ivy and window boxes that drip with colour. It's the prettiest house on the street with a surprisingly stylish interior; it's bright and airy, quietly funky, warm and pretty. Having been recently revived from top to toe there is much to impress: a fantastic breakfast room in light contemporary style with huge windows that flood the room with light; a sitting room in soothing purples, with good sofas, the odd oil painting and books on Hockney and Van Gogh. Bedrooms are not particularly large, but indulge nonetheless. You get loads of colour – yellows and purples, reds and creams, blues and greys – and rooms are spotless: stylishly uncluttered, not a nasty thing in sight. Smart shower rooms have green mosaic tiles, glass-bowl sinks and chrome fittings. Steal away across the road to sit in the communal gardens or play tennis on its courts. Don't miss Depa for great Indian food; the *Good Food Guide* food critic eats there every week. Covent Garden and the British Museum are walkable. A great price, too.

rooms	44: 18 singles, 9 doubles, 5 twins, 9 triples, 3 quadruples.
price	£95. Triples £105. Quadruples £110. Singles £75.
meals	Full English breakfast included.
closed	Never.
train	King's Cross; Euston.
tube	Russell Square; King's Cross; Euston.
bus	59, 68, 91, 168.

	Mary Burt
tel	020 7387 1551
fax	020 7387 4616
e-mail	book@harlingfordhotel.com
web	www.harlingfordhotel.com

Hotel

Map 2 Entry 108

The Generator

Compton Place, 37 Tavistock Place, Russell Square, London WC1H 9SE

A futuristic-film-set feel, with metal sculptures, blue neon light, *Clockwork Orange* wall hangings, and value for money at every turn. *Blade Runner* meets *Lonely Planet* at this central London hostel that's won all the awards a hostel can win. Breakfast is included, you can get fish and chips for £3, and cocktails in the bar at happy hour (6pm–9pm) are £2.50 a pop. There's a reading room with internet access, video games and a juke box in an 'industrial' bar where everything is metal and the lights all blue. The place can sleep up to 800 people so there's always someone about, and staff are friendly and helpful. You can buy London guides, phone cards, plug adaptors, even plane tickets. Bedrooms are basic: bed, duvet, sheets, towel, carpet, sink and locker, but all are clean, and if there are four of you, you can pay as little as £20 a night each and get a room to yourselves. Dorm beds cost even less. Even the bathrooms (piping hot water 24 hours a day) have been 'funked up'. A second Generator has opened in Berlin, a third is on the cards for Amsterdam. If none of the above puts you off, you'll love it.

rooms	217: A mix of twins, triples, quads, 5-bed, 6-bed, 8-bed and 14-bed dormitory rooms, with shower blocks on each floor.
price	Dorms £10–£17 p.p. Twin rooms £18–£25 p.p.
meals	Continental breakfast included; full English £3. Dinner from £3.
closed	Never.
tube	Russell Square.
bus	59, 68, 91, 168.

	Louise Duffy
tel	020 7388 7666
fax	020 7388 7644
e-mail	info@the-generator.co.uk
web	www.generatorhostels.com

Hostel

Map 2 Entry 109

The Rookery

12 Peter's Lane, Cowcross Street, Farringdon, London EC1M 6DS

A sublime country house in the heart of medieval London, a great retreat from the hustle of the Square Mile. The Rookery dates to 1764 and basks in the glow of graceful Georgian interiors, all of which are original, many of which were imported into the house. Walk in through the front door and immediately the scent of furniture wax assails you. Wander at will and you pass ancient panelling, pedimented mirrors, busts on plinths, old oils on the walls. In the drawing room there are leather sofas and old radiators, an honesty bar and French windows onto a small terraced garden, where stone urns brim with colour. Bedrooms are delightful, crisply elegant, uncluttered, yet full of beautiful things. You get carved half-testers, tall four-posters, period shutters and massive armoires. Exceptional bathrooms come with claw-foot baths, reclaimed sinks and Victorian, brass-piped showers. For the lap of luxury try the Rook's Nest, an enormous suite over two levels with views across the city's skyline; you bathe in the presence of a (stone) maiden. Kind staff and peace and quiet at night add the final touch. Wonderful.

rooms	33: 26 doubles, 6 singles, 1 suite.
price	£285–£325. Suite £580. Singles £250.
meals	Continental breakfast £9.75.
closed	Never.
train	Farringdon.
tube	Farringdon; St Paul's.
bus	8, 11, 15, 63, 76 242.

	Andy Broadman
tel	020 7336 0931
fax	020 7336 0932
e-mail	reservations@rookery.co.uk
web	www.rookeryhotel.com

Hotel

Map 2 Entry 110

Great Eastern Hotel
Liverpool Street, London EC2M 7QN

A thrilling hotel, an architectural masterpiece, a perfect fusion of classical and contemporary styles. It's a tale of three centuries. Built in 1884 as a grand response to the high days of train travel, the hotel prospered, only to fall into decline in the 1970s. It was rescued in 2000 and rebuilt in super-sleek style, with an atrium that rises seven floors high and a rotunda that circles up to a glass dome. All the jaw-dropping Victorian grandeur has been majestically restored – the sweeping marble staircase, the mosaic floors, a stupendous stained-glass dome in one of four dining rooms. Design comes from the 21st-century, with American oak panelling, leather and chrome chairs, furry bean bags and great modern art. Bedrooms have big beds, coloured throws, Egyptian linen, fluffy bath-robes; there are walls of wood, black and white photographs and a full hi-tech menu, too. This is a huge hotel; follow your nose and pass wonderful things, be it the Doric columns on the way to the champagne bar, the panelled walls in the hotel pub or the Egyptian masonic ceiling in the gym. *Weekend rates from £165.*

rooms	267: 16 singles, 200 doubles, 30 studios, 21 suites.
price	£310-£335. Singles £265. Suites from £395. Studios £370.
meals	Breakfast £7-£12. Lunch & dinner £10-£60. Room service.
closed	Never.
train	Liverpool Street (to Stansted).
tube	Liverpool Street.
bus	26, 28, 100, 242.

	Nicholas Rettie
tel	020 7618 5000
fax	020 7618 5011
e-mail	reservations@great-eastern-hotel.co.uk
web	www.great-eastern-hotel.co.uk

Hotel

Map 2 Entry 111

south

- **South Bank:** 60s complex housing the National Royal Theatre, National Film Theatre, Hayward Gallery and Royal Festival Hall

- **Tate Modern; Imperial War Museum; Design Museum; London Eye**

- **Royal Botanic Gardens, Kew:** reachable in summer by boat from Westminster Pier

- **Richmond Park:** woods, ponds, cycling tracks, bikes for hire, deer

- **Greenwich:** park, Royal Observatory, Cutty Sark, National Maritime Museum, ferry from Westminster Pier

- **Clapham:** trendy mix of Georgian and Victorian residences around the Common

- **Battersea:** lively shops, restaurants, bars and good old-fashioned park with zoo

- **Balham and Streatham:** up and coming residential areas with the open spaces of three commons

- **Putney and Barnes:** riverside spots, the latter with a village atmosphere

- **London Wetlands Centre:** bitterns return to London

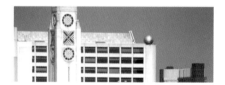

London Bridge Hotel

8-18 London Bridge Street, London SE1 9GS

The Romans built a bridge here in 400AD, probably earlier. Kings entered London over it – Olaf of Norway in 1014, John of France in 1357, Henry V on his way back from Agincourt. Check in here for a day or two and you, too, will feel like a king (or queen). Step off the street and you enter a haven of peace, a smart lobby with classical busts, soft marble floors and a couple of carved wooden plinths that flank the big, wooden fireplace. This is a smart hotel with excellent deals at weekends (Friday to Sunday), when, for under £150, you can bask in the contemporary splendour of one of the fancier rooms. You get cool interiors: neutral colours, huge beds, fibre-optic lighting, suede armchairs, classical prints, American oak panelling, plantation shutters and shiny granite bathrooms. The studios are bigger, with sofas and splashy oils, the apartments and enormous sitting rooms. There's a sauna in the gym, a funky bar next door and an excellent Malayo-Chinese restaurant in colonial style. Don't miss Borough Market, Tate Modern or Tower Bridge.

rooms	138: 132 twins/doubles, 3 studios, 3 apartments.
price	£190-£235; studios £270; apartments £325.
meals	Continental breakfast included; full English £13.95. Lunch & dinner £5-£35.
closed	Never.
train	London Bridge (to Gatwick); Liverpool Street (to Stansted).
tube	London Bridge.
bus	21, 35, 40, 43, 48, 133, 149, 343

	Nicholas Cowall
tel	020 7855 2200
fax	020 7855 2233
e-mail	sales@london-bridge.co.uk
web	www.londonbridgehotel.com

Hotel

Map 2 Entry 112

King's College London

Stamford Street Apartments, 127 Stamford Street, Waterloo, London SE1 9NQ

A university hall of residence, this one belonging to King's College London. It stands just around the corner from Waterloo Bridge, with the South Bank a short stroll (don't miss the National Film Theatre). The front of the building is listed (it was once the main London warehouse for WH Smiths) and it's a treat for singles: central, well-priced and incredibly secure (every door you go through needs a swipe card). Individual blocks are entered from a large central courtyard. Rooms are simple: clean and private with bed, carpet, desk, fridge, good storage and a shower. You are housed in 'flats', with about seven rooms sharing a private entrance and a communal kitchen; you can cook, watch TV, gather to chat. No cutlery or crockery (bring your own), but 24-hour porters, a daily maid service and a café in the main College building across the road open for the holidays (and gym and laundry). Waterloo station (and Eurostar) is a three-minute walk, and you can follow the Thames past the London Eye, up to Tate Modern, then over the millennium footbridge to St Paul's.

rooms	543 singles.
price	£33–£35.
meals	Full kitchen facilities provided.
closed	Open during summer holidays (July to mid-September) only.
train	Waterloo (Eurostar).
tube	Waterloo.
bus	1, 4, 26, 59, 68, 76, 168, 171.

	Kathryn Baron
tel	020 7848 1700
fax	020 7848 1717
e-mail	vacations@kcl.ac.uk
web	www.kcl.ac.uk/kcvb

University Hall of Residence

Map 2 Entry 113

The Bowling Hall

346 Kennington Road, London SE11 4LD

An artist, an architect and a bowling hall... This was once an Irish drinking den, a leap of the imagination that will confound the most agile of minds; it is now a pristine wonderland of cool lines and soothing colours. The feel is warm, uncluttered, hugely airy. The mix of old and new is delicious: rugs on limestone tiles, a satin wood chest, the tusk of a swordfish, wonderful old prints. Peter has renovated with huge style. Stand at the front door and look through the whole house. Hall, kitchen, sitting room – the view floats seamlessly through each room, 160 feet deep. On the walls, dazzling art, much of it Katherine's (the sitting room occasionally doubles as a gallery for her much-prized work). There are old books, collages, Byzantine urns. Bedrooms at the front of the house are simpler, with maple wood floors, linen curtains, light colours, the odd piece of art. You get the front of the house to yourself, including a mirrored bathroom and a sitting room that opens onto a gorgeous courtyard garden (bamboo, eucalyptus, pots of lavender). Cleaver Square, Borough market and the South Bank are all close.

rooms	2: 1 double, 1 single sharing shower/bath (same-party bookings only).
price	£80. Singles £45-£50.
meals	Continental breakfast included.
closed	Occasionally.
tube	Oval; Kennington.
bus	3, 36, 59, 159, 333.

	Peter Camp & Katherine Virgils
tel	020 7840 0454
fax	020 7840 0454
e-mail	bowlinghall@freenet.co.uk

B&B

 Map 5 Entry 114

12 Richborne Terrace
Oval, London SW8 1AU

A hop and a skip over Vauxhall Bridge, then a three-minute stroll to the tube at Oval; come for the test match and you could be in your seat within five minutes of closing the front door. What's more, you could take your own picnic. This is a super little find, with the whole of the top floor given over to guests who wish to self-cater. It's a bargain, too – not grand, but homely, and Leicester Square five stops away on the tube. You get your own sitting room in rainbow colours, with pretty armchairs and a sofa, a small dining room table, loads of books, and a TV. There are two bedrooms (thus great for families), with a pink single at the front and a small but comfy twin in green at the back (you can see the Oval's famous gasometer from the window). A well-stocked kitchen on the landing has oven, hobs, microwave, kettle, toaster, and there's a family-style bathroom in which to soak after a hard day in town. Sarah and Richard are the loveliest people. They assure your privacy, but go the extra mile and will happily do your shopping before you arrive (and charge nothing extra). Brilliant.

rooms	2: 1 double, 1 single.
price	£50. Singles £30.
meals	Self-catering; full kitchen facilities.
closed	Occasionally.
tube	Oval.
bus	3, 36, 59, 133, 155, 159, 185.

	Sarah & Richard Wells
tel	020 7582 2882

Self-Catering

Map 5 Entry 115

Rival

PO Box 4553, Henley-on-Thames, Oxfordshire RG9 3XZ

'Rival', a 1925 Luxmotor barge, spent her working life on Dutch canals, but in retirement crossed the channel and fell into Michael's hands. He gave her a makeover, top to toe. She now shines: varnished mahogany interiors, the original wheel in the wheelhouse, a woodburner in the saloon, even heated towel rails in compact shower rooms. A real sense of adventure – the high seas close to the high street (well, almost). 'Rival' is moored in London from October to March at Greenland Dock, Canada Water, and you can stay for B&B. Old cranes hang over the water, coots and swans come to bathe, Canary Wharf soars into the sky. Bring bikes and you can follow the river into town, past Tate Modern, the Festival Hall, the London Eye – just magical. In summer, she heads to Henley and messes about on the river. Here you can B&B or cruise from Hampton Court to Oxford. Breakfast on deck, stop at pubs for lunch, walk the Thames path – whatever you like. As for Frances, she was senior British springboard diving champion at the age of 12 and went to the Tokyo Olympics; like 'Rival', incredible.

rooms	3: 2 double cabins, 1 twin cabin. For group cruises a double sofabed is available.	
price	B&B: £80-£95. Singles from £60. Group cruises from £75 per person per day for B&B. Special itinaries by arrangement.	
meals	Full English breakfast included.	
closed	Occasionally.	
tube	Surrey Quays; Canada Water.	
bus	47, 188, 381.	

	Michael Clayton-Smith & Frances Northcott
tel	07976 390 416
e-mail	rivalbarge@orange.net
web	www.rivalbarge.com

B&B

Map 6 Entry 116

Hamilton House Hotel

14 West Grove, Greenwich, London SE10 8QT

Lady Hamilton, Nelson's mistress, lived here, so did Twining, as in the tea. Legend has it he used to sit on the balcony and watch his ships sail up the Thames, cup in hand. The balcony in question belongs to one of the bedrooms, and the huge view from it is the finest in this book, with Canary Wharf, the Thames and the City spread out like a picnic below: magnificent. On the other side of the house, step out the front door and you land on Blackheath; stroll across it to Greenwich Park, the Royal Observatory, the Meridian Line and the National Maritime Museum, then pick up a ferry and head to Westminster. As for the hotel, it's as good as you'd hope, with an airy elegance throughout. Come for stripped wood floors, voile curtains, original 1734 panelling and an exquisite tiled entrance hall. Wander out into the walled garden at night and find candlelit lanterns and fairy lights twinkling in the trees. Bedrooms are big and warm, decorated in pastel colours, with ornate fireplaces, huge beds and quilted throes. Or, come to get married; many do (just make sure you book a year in advance). The food's good, too.

rooms	9: 5 doubles, 4 four-posters.
price	£120-£150. Singles £100.
meals	Full English breakfast included. Dinner, 3 courses, £30. Room service.
closed	Never.
train	Greenwich.
tube	Greenwich.
bus	53, 177, 180.

	Karyn Halifax
tel	020 8694 9899
fax	020 8694 2370
e-mail	reception@hamiltonhousehotel.co.uk
web	www.hamiltonhousehotel.co.uk

Hotel

Map 6 Entry 117

113 Pepys Road
New Cross, London SE14 5SE

East meets west at Pepys Road. Anne is originally from Borneo, Tim was 'our man in East Malaysia'. They have travelled widely, are full of life, and now live on the side of a hill above a carpet of London lights. Hats on the hat stand, old maps and batiks on the walls. Anne has spared no expense in the decoration of her home and it sparkles. The downstairs room is worthy of an expensive hotel: the plushest of carpets, the biggest of beds, the crispest linen... There are bamboo blinds, Chinese screens, porcelain lamps and lacquered panels. Kimonos hang in the wardrobe, the bathroom is a monument to marble. Upstairs are two more bedrooms, one in country-house style, the other in contemporary yellow; both are lovely, airy and elegant, and the top-floor bathroom is a delight. There are orchids everywhere – Anne loves them. She also cooks brilliantly and will do you a steaming hot oriental cooked breakfast or the 'full English'. If you eat in at night, you might get smoked salmon, roast grouse and chocolate pudding. It's a short walk downhill for bus, tube and train. Don't miss the garden.

rooms	3: 1 double, 1 twin/double; 1 twin with separate bath.
price	£90. Singles £55.
meals	Full English breakfast included (oriental breakfast by arrangement). Dinner, by arrangement, £26 (BYO).
closed	Occasionally.
train	New Cross Gate (to London Bridge).
tube	New Cross Gate.
bus	21, 36, 53, 171, 172, 343.

	Anne & Tim Marten
tel	020 7639 1060
fax	020 7639 8780
e-mail	annemarten@pepysroad.com
web	www.pepysroad.com

B&B

Map 6 Entry 118

Shepherd's

39 Marmora Road, East Dulwich, London SE22 0RX

Watch out for Brian's homemade biscuits – they are profoundly sinful and impossible to resist. A quirky little place, just over a mile from the unmissable Dulwich Picture Gallery, which dates back to the 1790s and was set up by the King of Poland. Bedrooms here are surprisingly flamboyant, with Indian wall hangings, silky gold bedspreads, colourful window boxes and wooden beds. There are rag-rolled walls, bold colours, rugs on stripped floors, plates of fruit with napkins and knives... and packs of playing cards. Brian will chauffeur you around London (or Britain) in his 1954 Inspector-Maigret-style Citröen: leather seats, wooden dashboard, running boards, long-lost style. A glass of wine or beer on arrival, a lovely big open-plan kitchen/dining room ("guests can see if we burn their breakfast"), and a different cooked dish every morning. You can eat in at night, too – fish soup, rack of lamb, chocolate pud, that sort of thing; weight-watchers beware. There's a grand piano and a coal fire in the sitting room, two dozy dogs and views over London. Station pick-ups and drop-offs, too.

rooms	4: 1 double; 2 doubles, 1 twin sharing 2 bathrooms (both bath & shower).
price	£60–£70. Singles from £50.
meals	Full English breakfast included. Dinner with wine £25; supper £10, by arrangement.
closed	Occasionally.
train	Honour Oak Park (to Victoria or London Bridge); West Dulwich (to Victoria).
bus	12, 63.

	Penny & Brian Shepherd
tel	020 8693 4355
fax	020 8693 7954
e-mail	dulwichdragon@hotmail.com
web	www.shepherdslondon.com

B&B

Map 6 Entry 119

24 Fox Hill

Crystal Palace, London SE19 2XE

Wander around at the top of the hill for views over London about 30 miles of them. Sue and Tim have renovated with style. They moved out of central London for the space, the trees, the sky… all of which you get here in abundance. Shades of the Raj as you enter, with old pictures of stern gentlemen in pith helmets (one of them Sue's grandfather). Then come the wall-hangings, some Sue's work – she is a graduate of Chelsea Art College and has a studio at the back. Inside: wooden floors, warm rugs, a Swedish stove in the sitting room, and a wall of books on the landing. Beautiful bedrooms are full of antiques and paintings; the biggest has a sofa and candelabra. At breakfast, sit at the kitchen table and look out onto the tree that Pissarro painted in 1870; then hop on a train and go see the painting – it hangs in the National Gallery. When you return, Sue will cook supper (sea bass, maybe, stuffed with herbs), or dine out nearby; you can eat your way around the world. There's a fantastic bookshop at the top of the hill and don't forget your walk in the park. Oh, and their lovely garden, too.

rooms	3: 1 twin/double; 1 double, 1 twin sharing shower.
price	£80–£100. Singles from £50.
meals	Full English breakfast included. Dinner £25–£30, by arrangement.
closed	Occasionally.
train	Crystal Palace (to Victoria or London Bridge).
bus	2, 3.

	Sue & Tim Haigh
tel	020 8768 0059
e–mail	suehaigh@foxhill-bandb.co.uk
web	www.foxhill-bandb.co.uk

B&B

Map 6 Entry 120

34 Ambleside Avenue
Streatham, London SW16 1QP

A beautiful pyracantha guards the front of this handsome 1880s red-brick house. There's history, too; Emily Pankhurst held meetings here, and the house once belonged to Carl Davis, the American film composer. A very friendly place and Chris and Viveka (who's Swedish) give generously of their space and time. There's a snug library-sitting room with fenders round the fire and a stylish dining room flanked by trompe l'oeil pillars. This is a smart family home with bedrooms that fit the bill: comfy beds, antique furniture, pretty fabrics, tartan blankets. Best of all is the enormous room at the top. It has space for a couple of sofas and twin beds hidden up in the eaves, making it perfect for families. In good weather late breakfasts on Sunday mornings can be taken in the pretty walled garden; bells may peel at next-door St Leonard's church (where concerts are sometimes held). Swedish or continental breakfasts come courtesy of Viveka, while Chris will pick you up from the station when you arrive; there's off-street parking, too. Famous Streatham sons include David Garrick, Joshua Reynolds and Dr Johnson.

rooms	3: 1 double with separate bathroom; 1 twin, 1 family sharing shower.
price	£60. Singles £45.
meals	Continental breakfast included.
closed	Occasionally.
train	Streatham (to London Bridge); Streatham Hill (to Victoria).
tube	Tooting Bec (10-minute walk).
bus	133, 159, 319.

	Viveka & Chris Collingwood
tel	020 8769 2742
fax	020 8677 3023
e-mail	info@bednbrek.com
web	www.bednbrek.com

B&B

Map 5 Entry 121

52 Becmead Avenue
Streatham, London SW16 1UQ

Supermodel Naomi Cambell grew up in Becmead Avenue. At Number 52 you'll find the models on the walls. Michael, an erstwhile Sotherby's autioneer, deals in fine art. He and Katherine lived for 17 years in Florence and Rome and their house brims with beautiful pictures, exquisite maps, gorgeous prints: more than just a little style. Equally surprising is the house itself; you don't usually expect to walk into a panelled hall in Streatham. Walls, floors and stairs – all are wood. It's very homely, a small-scale country house. Bedrooms have the same style. Original tiled fireplaces come in different colours: turquoise in the four-poster, fire-engine red in the double. There are lots of books, rugs on floors, crisp linen and garden views. One bathroom has a colourful mural of underwater life, though plans to redecorate are in the air. This is very much a family home and breakfast around a long oak farmhouse table in a big open-plan kitchen/dining room. Katherine will cook the full works or you can go continental and have cheese and ham. She also makes her own marmalade, but you'll have to beat Michael to it. A very friendly place.

rooms	3: 1 double with separate bath; 1 double with separate shower; 1 single sharing shower.
price	£60-£65. Singles from £35.
meals	Full English breakfast included.
closed	Occasionally.
train	Streatham (to London Bridge); Streatham Hill (to Victoria).
tube	Brixton (10 minutes by bus).
bus	57, 133, 159, 319.

	Katherine & Michael Thomson-Glover
tel	020 8696 0107
fax	020 8677 4552
e-mail	katherinetg@tiscali.co.uk

B&B

Map 5 Entry 122

38 Killieser Avenue

Streatham, London SW2 4NT

Few people do things with as much natural good humour and style as Winkle. The Haworths – early Streatham pioneers – have brought country-house chic to South London. The house glows 'mellow yellow', and there are flowers in every room; muted pinks, lilacs, blues. You breakfast in the rug-strewn, wooden-floored, farmhouse kitchen, but can decamp in spring or summer to the spectacular garden: agapanthus, pink wisteria, roses by the dozen, tulips and jasmine – 20 years of dedicated hard work, a splendid spot for bacon and eggs. At the front door, umbrellas, tennis rackets and a grandfather clock. Upstairs, big bedrooms are grand and homely: more rugs, lamb's wool blankets, loads of books, waffle bathrobes, beautiful linen on superb matresses: Winkle does nothing by halves. There's a generous single, with a writing desk, a large armchair and views onto this quiet residential street. Streatham Hill station is a three-minute walk; you can be in Victoria in 15 minutes, but even if it took an hour, it'd be worth the trouble. Brilliant.

rooms	2: 1 twin, 1 single sharing bath.
price	£80-£90. Singles £50-£60.
meals	Full English breakfast included. Dinner, by arrangement, £25.
closed	Occasionally.
train	Streatham Hill (to Victoria).
tube	Balham (15-minute walk).
bus	45, 57, 58, 137, 159, 319.

	Winkle Haworth
tel	020 8671 4196
fax	020 8761 4196
e-mail	winklehaworth@hotmail.com

B&B

Map 5 Entry 123

39 Telford Avenue
Streatham Hill, London SW2 4XL

A very pretty home, a real family enclave, with children doing homework at the kitchen table (or watching TV). An exceptionally welcoming place, with a fire in the hall on a cold February afternoon, and tea and home-baked cakes waiting in the kitchen. Richard, an architect, oversaw a total renovation, hence the smooth lines and warm style that fill the house. There are wooden floors and lime green walls in the hall, a church pew and a piano in the airy dining room. Here you breakfast heartily at a big farmhouse table, with a woodburner to keep you warm and lovely big French windows looking onto the back garden (you might spot the local fox). The whole house is wonderfully restful, stylish homely, with bright colours, pretty furniture and fresh flowers everywhere. The bedroom is at the front. It has a sofa, an ornate fireplace, a wall of books, black and white photographs above the bed and fleeced blankets in blue and green. The bathroom, two paces across the landing, comes in electric pink. There's off-street parking for those who need it, and a washing machine you're free to use.

rooms	1 twin/double with separate bath.
price	£60. Singles £30.
meals	Full English breakfast included.
closed	Occasionally.
train	Streatham Hill (to Victoria).
tube	Balham (10-minute walk); Brixton (10-minute bus ride).
bus	59, 109, 118, 133, 137, 159, 250.

	Katharine & Richard Wolstenholme
tel	020 8674 4343
fax	020 8678 6667
e-mail	rwolstenholme@aol.com

B&B

Map 5 Entry 124

108 Streathbourne Road

Balham, London SW17 8QY

In the hall on the wall, a great aunt (well, her portrait)...? This is an Aussie-English partnership, Mary being a Sydneysider who has infiltrated Parliament. Their 1880 terraced home is in a quiet tree-lined street, part of a conservation area. Tooting Common is at the end of the road and its lido – something of a South London institution – is supposedly the largest in the world (or coldest?). Exercise freaks can head off pre-breakfast, do their lengths, then return to find a fire in the dining room and defrost. You get the newspaper, too, and if the weather's good, French windows open up to a pretty London garden. Pots of geraniums sit on the window ledge outside the bedroom; inside you find an armchair, a writing desk, fresh flowers and a big comfy walnut bed. Sheets and blankets or duvets – whatever you want; a very pretty room. There's a twin room upstairs, so you can bring the children (or they can bring you). Nick Jones (of Soho House) has just opened the Balham Kitchen and the locals are flocking in. There's Dish Dash for great Persian cooking, too. *Minimum stay two nights.*

rooms	2: 1 double with separate bath; 1 twin sharing bath (same party bookings only). Minimum stay two nights.
price	£65-£75. Singles from £55.
meals	Full English breakfast included. Dinner, by arrangement, £25.
closed	Occasionally.
train	Balham (to Victoria).
tube	Balham; Tooting Bec.
bus	155, 319.

	Mary & David Hodges
tel	020 8767 6931
fax	020 8672 8839
e-mail	mary.hodges@virgin.net
web	www.streathbourneroad.com

B&B

Map 5 Entry 125

The Coach House

2 Tunley Road, Balham, London SW17 7QJ

This was home to the man who built the street and he built himself a coach house, too… for which you will thank him as it is now a very pretty studio at the back of the house. Meena and Harley came here four years ago and have renovated completely, with Meena, a gardener/interior designer, making sure that both inside and outside scrubbed up brilliantly. In the main house, shiny wooden floors, loads of rugs and the odd exotic touch, while outside, a delightful courtyard garden with a pergola, a fountain, Indian sandstone paving and various fruit trees (peach, pear, nectarine). Breakfast, a feast, is taken in the main house ("I do the cooking, Harley does the talking"), and five-course evening meals start with "the ceremony of the sherry" before "starter, soup, fish, meat, cheese and fruit" so don't expect to go hungry. The coach house is decorated in country style. The room under the eaves is open to the rafters, French windows open onto flowers, and there are *toile de Jouy* fabrics, rugs on wooden floors and masses of space. It's all yours, very pretty, very quiet and close to the tube.

rooms	2: 1 family, 1 twin. Same-party bookings only.
price	£100 for 2; £135 for 3; £150 for 4; £165 for 5.
meals	Full English breakfast included. Dinner £45, by arrangement (5 courses).
closed	Occasionally.
train	Balham (to Victoria).
tube	Balham.
bus	155, 319.

	Meena & Harley Nott
tel	020 8772 1939
fax	0870 133 4957
e-mail	coachhouse@chslondon.com
web	www.coachhouse.chslondon.com

B&B

Map 4 Entry 126

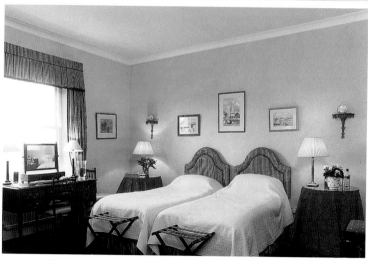

22 Northbourne Road

Clapham Common, London SW4 7DJ

Past Clapham residents include Captain Cook, Samuel Pepys and William Wilberforce. Hardacanute, King of England (1040-1042), attended a wedding here, overdid the wine a bit, and expired. A village for 700 years, Clapham still keeps a sense of being apart from the rest of London. After the Great Fire it became fashionable to live here. It still is, hence all the grand houses, of which this is one. It dates to the mid-1800s. Bay trees stand guard behind smart black railings at the front, where wandering lavender adds a touch of colour. Inside, you get county-house charm: old oils and a marble fireplace in the drawing room, a mahogany table in the dining room and a 160-foot back garden, patrolled, occasionally, by two (lazy) border terriers. Upstairs past the ski suits (Libby sells them) you find a large, elegant room. Expect fresh flowers, plush fabrics, bowls of fruit, a pretty dressing table, lots of books and lots of space. The common is close and if you want to take the bus into town, the 88 passes Tate Britain, Big Ben, Downing Street and Trafalgar Square.

rooms	2: 1 twin/double, 1 occasional single, sharing bath (same-party bookings only).
price	£80. Singles from £50.
meals	Full English breakfast included.
closed	Occasionally.
tube	Clapham Common.
bus	88, 137, 345.

	Libby & Clive de Rougemont
tel	020 7720 4871
fax	020 7622 6803
e-mail	cliveder@tinyworld.co.uk

B&B

Map 5 Entry 127

20 St Philip Street
Battersea, London SW8 3SL

Barbara's tiny garden is something of a hit with guests and you may find yourself out here enjoying a summer sundowner. It is full of life – hanging baskets, arum lilies, wandering jasmine – a very soothing spot. Not that the rest of the house is anything but. This is a delightful, double-fronted, terraced cottage, built in 1890 by the Peabody Trust. Barbara, who spoils you rotten, pretty much gives you the run of the place. You breakfast in the dining room by the original Victorian fireplace, while across the hall there's a lovely sitting room with gilt-framed mirrors, wooden blinds, a plump-cushioned sofa, and a piano (which you are welcome to play). Upstairs, two very comfy bedrooms come with padded headboards, thick curtains, pretty linen, books, guides, mirrors – nothing has been overlooked. The next-door bathroom is fabulous with porthole windows, a huge mirror and a radio to entertain you as you soak. You have wonderful Battersea Park to the north, and Clapham Common, with its fishing lake, to the south. Good for the Chelsea Flower Show, too.

rooms	2: 1 double with separate bath & shower; 1 double sharing bath (same party bookings only).
price	£70-£80. Singles £50-£60.
meals	Full English breakfast included.
closed	Occasionally.
train	Queenstown Road (to Waterloo); Battersea Park (to Victoria).
bus	137.

	Barbara Graham
tel	020 7498 9967
fax	020 7498 9967
e-mail	stay@bed-breakfast-battersea.co.uk
web	www.bed-breakfast-battersea.co.uk

B&BOther Place

Map 5 Entry 128

Worfield Street
Battersea, London SW11 4RB

A skip and a jump over Albert Bridge (the pretty one with the lights, which appears in all the films) and you are in deepest Chelsea and the pleasure-dome of the King's Road. On your doorstep is Battersea Park, with lake, zoo, bandstand, pagoda, riverside walk and a tremendous firework display each November 5th. Catriona's 1880 Victorian terraced home is a great find: very pretty and excellent value for money. You get the huge room at the top to yourselves, with sky-lights on each side, making it bright, light and colourful. There's masses of space and great modern art on the walls (the work of Catriona's son), wooden floors covered with rugs, a rocking chair and bright cushions on the sofa (it turns into a bed and can easily cope with a couple of small children). Breakfast is a movable feast: you can either have it in bed or down in the kitchen. Catriona will also cook you supper, if you want – maybe spaghetti bolognese or roast chicken. Alternatively, there are lots of local restaurants: the Duke of Cambridge is excellent, especially its Sunday lunch. There's jazz in the park in summer, too.

rooms	1 double (with double sofabed) with separate shower.
price	£80. Singles £50.
meals	Continental breakfast included. Supper £10, by arrangement.
closed	Occasionally.
bus	19, 49, 319, 345.

	Catriona & Michael Bradley
tel	020 7223 1243
e-mail	michael_bradley@ukgateway.net

B&B

Map 4 Entry 129

33 The White House

Vicarage Crescent, Battersea Village, London SW11 3LJ

This is a very pretty apartment down by the river past Battersea Bridge, a touch far-flung (but only a touch), yet terrifically peaceful, thus well worth the bother. The White House is a 1930s apartment block with a landscaped courtyard on the inside, where trees reach for the skies and window boxes tumble with colour. Helen's pad is up on the first floor. Walk in though the front door and you are greeted with a clipped English elegance (Helen is a Dane at home in London). Beautiful art hangs on the walls, light floods in through myriad windows and antique mahogany dressers shine. The main bedroom is large, with an armchair in the corner, cushions on a comfy bed and 16 pictures on one wall. There's a very pretty twin in lilac with delicate floral duvets, an elegantly snug sitting room with comfy sofas and a round dining table in the dining hall. A lovely place, impeccably stylish, quite small, very well laid-out. For £120 a night, you can have the whole place to yourselves. Buses will whizz you over the bridge to the King's Road in five minutes, but don't miss Battersea Park, where you can walk by the river.

rooms	2: 1 twin, 1 double sharing bath (same-party bookings only).
price	£65. Singles £45.
meals	Full English breakfast included.
closed	Occasionally.
train	Clapham Junction (to Gatwick).
bus	239.

	Helen Knowles
tel	020 7223 7561
e-mail	helenknowles33@aol.com

33 Barmouth Road
Wandsworth Common, London SW18 2DT

Great value for money down at Wandsworth Common, so splash out at nearby Chez Bruce, one of London's gastronomic crown jewels. Nessie (a fashion designer) and Duncan (a sports editor on a national daily) were in the throes of finishing a total renovation, and although their home was not complete when we visited, B&B runs in their blood; this is going to be a great place to stay: very comfortable, nicely priced, with easy-going natives. It's a smart 1880s terraced house of which only the exterior walls survive; everything else is new, from the four flights of stairs to the Farrow & Ball paints. Expect neutral colours, a clipped cosy elegance, old pine dressers and Aga-cooked breakfasts. Stone-flagged floors in the enormous kitchen are kept warm with underfloor heating, there are creamy walls, a pretty Arts-and-Crafts feel and curtains made by Nessie. Uncluttered bedrooms at the top of the house have good linen, soothing colours, modem points and TVs. Check out the web site as things will change, but expect to feel very at home. The Maclays have a young family, which is about to expand.

rooms	2 twins/doubles.
price	£50. Singles £35.
meals	Full English breakfast included.
closed	Occasionally.
train	Wandsworth Town or Clapham Junction (both via Vauxhall).
tube	Tooting Bec (5-minute bus ride).
bus	77, 77A, 219.

	Nessie & Duncan Maclay
tel	020 8877 0331
e-mail	b&b@maclayworld.com
web	www.maclayworld.com

B&B

Map 4 Entry 131

9 Clarendon Drive
Putney, London SW15 1AW

Jane wears various hats – basket-maker, painter, B&B – but the day I visited, she'd cooked lunch for 80 vicars at the church hall. A very down-to-earth place. There are hockey sticks and tennis rackets by the front door, lovely pictures on the walls and a garden with two ponds and the odd resident frog. Upstairs, you find warm bedrooms full of lovely wood furniture. One has an ancient pine dresser, the other is cosily tucked up in the eaves (the second staircase is for the the nimble-footed). You get TVs and radios, soft colours, colourful linen and piles of magazines. The feel is homely – smart without being posh, simple without being scruffy – a very comfortable place to stay. Downstairs a big, airy kitchen/dining room comes in country style (stripped wood floors, lots of art, high ceilings, huge windows). Jane chats over breakfast, which is devoured around a large square mahogany table. Head down to Putney Embankment (the Boat Race starts here) and follow the towpath along the river up to Hammersmith – it's one of London's loveliest walks.

rooms	2 twins sharing bath & shower.
price	£55–£60. Singles £35–£40.
meals	Continental breakfast included.
closed	Occasionally.
train	Putney (to Waterloo via Vauxhall).
tube	East Putney.
bus	14, 22.

	Jane Theophilus
tel	020 8789 3144
e-mail	janetheo@amserve.net

B&B

Map 4 Entry 132

3 Briar Walk

Putney, London SW15 6UD

I will not do justice to Briar Walk in 200 words, but I can tell you this: Phyllis and Tremayne are the loveliest of people – down-to-earth and full of life. They stop and chat with easy grace, which is why I cannot describe the dining room, as the conversation flowed so effortlessly that we forgot to take a look. A house of stars, too. Andy Roddick stayed as a Wimbledon junior, as did Vladimir Kramnick when he defeated Kasparov in 2000 (Tremayne was his team leader). As for Tremayne, he played rugby for Scotland ('58-'64), yet he and Phyllis are stars of equal brightness, and Phyllis looks after you with generosity of spirit making this a very happy family home. And some family it is, too. Walk upstairs and pass the portrait of James Rennell (he discovered the Gulf Stream), while one of Tremayne's uncles was married to Nancy Mitford. Tremayne loves games, so get back early for the Briar Walk evening croquet match or perhaps a hand of racing demon. Rooms are warm, homely, grand and rambling, slightly cluttered with lovely aristocratic junk, but it's the easy-going natives who make this house so special.

rooms	3: 1 studio for 2 with kitchen; 1 twin; 1 single with separate bathroom.
price	£75-£85. Singles £35-£40.
meals	Continental breakfast included.
closed	Occasionally.
train	Barnes (to Waterloo via Vauxhall).
tube	East Putney (20-minute walk).
bus	14, 37, 74, 337.

	Tremayne & Phyllis Rennell of Rodd
tel	020 8785 2338
fax	020 8785 7338
e-mail	tremrod@aol.com
web	www.briarwalkbnb.com

B&B

Map 3 Entry 133

106 Elm Grove Road
Barnes, London SW13 0BS

This is a lovely 1900 Edwardian terraced home with lots of original features – the tiles in the entrance hall, the marble fireplace – but the feel here is distinctly fresh: bright and breezy country chic. At the back of the house, the enormous open-plan kitchen/dining room has a conservatory roof, flooding the room with light. There are creamy walls, duck-egg-blue cupboards and a round dining table for big breakfast which Nigel cooks and serves on blue china. Bedrooms upstairs are all different, all lovely. The big twin at the front has a huge gilt mirror resting on a walnut dresser, the double at the back has a French wooden bed. You get pure cotton linen, carafes of water, pretty rugs, maybe a writing desk. Rooms up in the eaves are cosy and spotless with velux windows, so if you're lucky you can fall asleep to the sound of the rain. A house of flowers, and art, too, courtesy of two daughters, one a florist, the other an art student. Wander up to Barnes village for antique shops, head to the Bull's Head for the best jazz, or pop over to Wimbledon for the tennis. The common is at the top of the road.

rooms	3: 1 twin; 1 double, 1 single sharing bath.
price	£70–£80. Singles £40–£45.
meals	Full English breakfast included. Dinner, 2 courses, £15.
closed	Occasionally.
train	Barnes (to Waterloo via Vauxhall)
tube	Hammersmith (7-minute bus ride).
bus	33, 72, 209, 283.

	Marie Therese Wilson & Nigel Viney
tel	020 8876 9033
fax	020 8412 9400
e-mail	mtbedandbreakfast@blueyonder.co.uk
web	www.barnesbedandbreakfast.co.uk

B&B

Map 3 Entry 134

The Victoria

10 West Temple Sheen, Richmond, London SW14 7RT

This is a cool, contemporary gastropub, that manages to be both down-to-earth and quietly vibrant. Big airy rooms are full of pretty things: expect Designers Guild leather armchairs, comfy sofas, Bonzini table football, painted floorboards and splashy modern oils. The locals love it and have turned it into a *de facto* community centre. Mothers gather for coffee after they've dropped off the kids off at school – but they come for the food, too, and for good reason. Mark and Clare have transformed the place in the three years they've been here; the hallmarks now are fine rooms, good food and helpful staff. Treat yourself to *caldo verde*, bouillabaisse, and poached pear with chocolate for about £25, then retire to stylish bedrooms. You'll find white walls, Egyptian cotton, beechwood beds, suede bedheads, goose down pillows, cashmere blankets and high-pressure showers. Every room has a PC and broadband internet connection… all free. Great value for money, and with the Sheen Gate entrance to Richmond Park close by, you can walk off your indulgence lost to the world. A great little place.

rooms	7: 5 doubles, 2 twins/doubles.
price	£99.50.
meals	Continental breakfast included. Lunch & dinner £10-£35.
closed	Christmas.
train	Mortlake (to Waterloo via Vauxhall).
bus	33, 337, 485.

	Mark Chester & Clare Lumley
tel	020 8876 4238
fax	020 8878 3464
e-mail	mark@thevictoria.net
web	www.thevictoria.net

Restaurant with Rooms

Map 3 Entry 135

131 Queens Road
Richmond, TW10 6HF

Margaret, a professional chef, runs cookery courses for beginners: women – send your husbands. Each course is tailor-made. She can teach him to cook all your favourites, so when he returns… (Is this The Yum-Yum Sisterhood?). Alternatively, she'll cook for you, maybe homemade coriander and carrot soup, rack of lamb, cold lemon soufflé – or tip you the wink on Richmond's best restaurants (the White Horse pub was causing local waistlines to expand). By day you can work up an appetite with trips to Windsor (there's a direct train) or Hampton Court (take the ferry and arrive like Henry VIII). If these destinations sound a little distant, just hop across the road for walks in Richmond Park – London's loveliest – or jump on the train to Waterloo; it only takes 12 minutes. At night, climb the stairs in this Richmond family home (1930s pebble dash with leaded bay windows) to a simple bedroom at the front, a room of blues and yellows warm as toast, books, blankets, double glazing – for a good night's sleep. Station pick-ups, good conversation and fine breakfasts to start your day.

rooms	1 twin with separate bath.
price	£70. Singles £45.
meals	Continental breakfast included. Dinner, £30, by arrangement.
closed	Occasionally.
train	Richmond (to Waterloo via Vauxhall).
tube	Richmond.
bus	33, 337, 485.

Margaret & Ian Andrew

tel	020 8948 6893
e-mail	mmandred131@aol.com

B&B

Map 3 Entry 136

Chalon House

8 Spring Terrace, Paradise Road, Richmond, Surrey TW9 1LW

Miniature conifers in terracotta pots stand guard in front of the windows of this 1740s Georgian house – good feng-shui, apparently. Ann does things impeccably: cheerful breakfasts around the smart dining table, a decanter of sherry from which to help yourself in the sitting room, umbrellas in the hall in case of rain. Best of all are the spotless bedrooms – big, bright, high-ceilinged – with original Georgian shutters and pine doors, maybe a shiny brass bed. One has lovely high windows; another has a private entrance and an enormous old fireplace. There are spoiling bathrooms (one has a claw-foot bath), bowls of fresh fruit and pretty furniture – all extremely civilised. You're in the heart of Richmond. You can strike out and wander old alleyways, watch cricket on the green or walk along the towpath by the river. The station is a five-minute walk, while Richmond Park is roughly a mile to the south and Kew Gardens a mile to the north. Ann, who came here via Italy and the Cape, also has green fingers and has brought her courtyard garden to life with busts and statues, a flowering cherry and pots by the dozen.

rooms	3: 1 double, 2 twins.
price	£80–£90. Singles £70.
meals	Full English breakfast included.
closed	Occasionally.
train	Richmond (to Waterloo via Vauxhall).
tube	Richmond.
bus	33, 190, 337.
tel	Ann & Virgilio Zaina
	020 8332 1121
e-mail	virgilioz@aol.com

Doughty Cottage
142A Richmond Hill, Richmond, Surrey TW10 6RN

You get a bit of theatre at Doughty. Climb the stone steps in the secret garden and you enter an Aladdin's Cave of Renaissance wonder. In the hall you find a Capo de Monte chandelier, a Barteloni wood carving, and a terracotta senorita holding a pot of silk flowers. Extraordinarily, it's the bedrooms in this 1750s Regency cottage (it once belonged to Sir Francis Cooke) that take the biscuit. There are murals in bathrooms, four-poster beds and exquisite hand-painted wardrobes. Every square inch is covered with something wonderful, be it busts on plinths, old oils on the walls or glistening chandeliers hanging from the ceiling. Thick regal curtains tumble, one of the bathrooms comes with a gilt-framed mirror. The two downstairs rooms have their own private gardens, so breakfast in summer surrounded by terracotta pots and the sweet smell of jasmine. The room at the top is huge, with ceilings open to the rafters and a view to feed the soul; a meandering river Thames at the bottom of the hill. Fabulous bathrooms, big fluffy towels, the works. Beautiful Richmond Park is a two-minute walk away.

rooms	3: 1 family, 1 twin/double; 1 double with separate bath.
price	£75-£98. Singles from £70
meals	Continental breakfast included.
closed	Occasionally.
train	Richmond (to Waterloo via Vauxhall).
tube	Richmond.
bus	65, 371.

	Denise & Greg O'Neill
tel	020 8332 9434
fax	020 8948 3716
e-mail	deniseoneill425@aol.com
web	www.doughtycottage.com

B&B

Map 3 Entry 138

Paddock Lodge
The Green, Hampton Court, London KT8 9BW

Hampton Court Palace, London's Tudor masterpiece, is at the end of the road. It was home to Henry VIII and remained a royal residence until George II, though perhaps if they'd known Paddock Lodge… This is a sublime country house with spectacular gardens that roll down to the River Thames, but Louis and Sonya are the real stars – kind and gentle with a great sense of humour, and they give generously of their Georgian/Edwardian home. There's a panelled snug in which to play the piano, a double-aspect dining room that floods with morning light and a wonderful drawing room where an open fire burns in winter (and where tea and delicious home-baked cakes are served every day). The main bedroom is huge, decorated beautifully in blues and whites, with river views, antique furniture and a panelled bathroom. The smaller bedroom has a brass bed and looks over the Royal Mews. Hire bikes and follow the Thames to Richmond Park, or drive to Kew, Windsor or Wisley. Hampton Court holds various festivals – music, flower, needlework – throughout the year. Wimbledon is close, London half an hour by train.

rooms	2: 1 double with bath; 1 double with separate bath.
price	£90–£100. Singles from £55.
meals	Full breakfast included. Dinner, 4 courses, £27.50, by arrangement (Jewish & continental cusine).
closed	Occasionally.
train	Hampton Court (to Waterloo).

	Dr Louis & Mrs Sonia Marks
tel	020 8979 5254
e-mail	paddocklodge@compuserve.com
web	www.paddocklodge.co.uk

B&B

Map 7 Entry 139

Heasleigh

239 Hook Road, Chessington, Surrey KT9 1EQ

One of the most surprising places in this book; you do not expect to find heaven behind a modest exterior on a busy road. Heasleigh is a house of two halves. Inside you find the loveliest of interiors, fresh and airy, with Farrow & Ball paints, pretty bedside tables, bowls of fruit and shiny parquet floors. Bedrooms are big, trim and uncluttered, with wicker chairs, stylish shower rooms and sunshine colours (greens, reds, yellows, blues). Then there's the small matter of what lies behind you, namely the jaw-dropping garden. I am no horticulturist and barely know a daisy from a daffodil, but this is clearly a masterpiece – Chessington's own Garden of Eden. Both bedrooms have doors into it; one has its own conservatory stuffed with pelargoniums, orchids, palms – just spectacular. Forage further and find a 190-foot-long garden that has been transformed from lawn and bed into a broad sweep of soft English colour, with a tunnel of roses and a potager... heavenly stuff. Bring back picnic suppers and eat out at night. Dawn's breakfasts are the icing on the cake. There's off-street parking, too.

rooms	2: 1 double, 1 twin/double.
price	£70. Singles from £45.
meals	Full English breakfast included.
closed	Occasionally.
train	Surbiton (to Waterloo).

	Derek and Dawn St Romaine
tel	020 8397 4187
fax	020 8397 4187
e-mail	dawn@gardenphotolibrary.com
web	www.gardenphotolibrary.com

B&B

Map 7 Entry 140

London pubs

A selection of special London pubs, taken from our new guide
Pubs & Inns of England and Wales.
Available through bookshops and from:
www.specialplacestostay.com.

Royal Inn on the Park

There are many fine pubs clustered around Victoria Park but none of them as enjoyable as this one. A massive Victorian local guarding the edge of the park, it has all the faded grandeur its name suggests; high ceilings, dark corners, open fires – a truly pubby feel. There's also a bar that can be hired for private functions. In summer it's fantastic, with a big covered seating area outside and a garden that backs the park: relax with the children and watch the world go by. The place buzzes in the evening with a mix of traditional characters and fashionable, though not achingly so, new East Enders. Chalked up on the menu is some tasty pub grub: salmon and sweet potato fishcakes, bacon and dolce latte risotto, rib steak. Puddings are a speciality. To drink… a well-kept real ale or one of 12 decent wines available by the glass. The jukebox that favours jazz and funk is usually drowned out by the volubility of the crowd as the evening fizzes towards closing time.

directions	Nearest tube: Mile End.
meals	12pm-3pm; 6pm-9.30pm; 12pm-9.30pm Saturdays; 12pm-5pm Sundays. No food Sunday evenings. Main courses £7.50-£12.

John Cheeseman
Royal Inn on the Park,
111 Lauriston Road,
Hackney, London E9 7HJ
tel 020 8985 3321

🚶 🍺 🍷

Map: 2 Entry: 141

Drapers Arms

The Islington Labour Party was founded in the meeting room upstairs. Islington, the Labour Party and The Drapers have come a long way in the 100-odd years since but they have travelled together and today's Labour group would be just as happy here as their forebears. In the old days, there was probably only beer, sandwiches and Clause 4 on the menu; today's deliberations are more likely to be accompanied by gnocchi with gorgonzola, spinach and pinenuts or perfect foie gras, washed down with an Amarone della Valpolicella at £65 a bottle. There are, of course, less pricey vintages on offer… and delicious roasts on Sundays. In a quiet side street off Upper Street, the once ramshackle Drapers has rejoiced in its renaissance ever since Paul McElhinney took over two years ago. It has won a hatful of awards for its food and is friendly, airy and scrupulously clean. A terrific place in which to settle down on a comfy leather sofa with a jug of Bloody Mary. Outside there's a lovely little garden for summer.

directions	Nearest tube: Highbury & Islington.
meals	12pm-3pm; 7pm-10.30pm. No food Sunday evenings. Main courses £9-£16.

Paul McElhinney
Drapers Arms,
44 Barnsbury Street,
Islington, London N1 1ER
tel 020 7619 0348

🚶 🍷

Map: 2 Entry: 142

The King's Head Theatre Pub

Dan Crawford set up London's first pub theatre decades ago in the then unfashionable Islington. All these years later, both he and it are still going strong. Indeed, the King's Head has an international reputation and has Tom Stoppard, Kenneth Branagh and Antony Sher among its ardent and vociferous supporters. Book in advance, have dinner, see the show – the newly-tarted up 115-seat theatre is upstairs and is huge fun. But don't think the pub plays second fiddle to the drama: it's a vibrant local with a late licence and jumps with live music every night. There's food for those who watch the show, real ales (Adnams, Young's) and a couple of wines by the glass. The King's Head is all about performance and the energy that goes with it, so there's a terrific buzz in the heaving, wooden-floored front bar, and a heady mix of students, Islington trendies, thesps and late-night revellers.

The House

There's been a transformation here. The old Belinda Castle has become The House, and every day brings another accolade. The chef is a Marco Pierre White protegée – people travel far for the cooking. Mirrors gleam on pale lemon walls, one slice of the wedge-shaped building is given over to white-clothed tables, candles and twinkly lights, the other is a chic and charming bar, with a real fire. Food is simple, gutsy, modern: try courgette and aubergine fritters, roast bream with trompette mushrooms, braised lentils and basil coulis, or good old shepherd's pie. Save space for pudding... treacle pudding, crème brulée, chocolate parfait. It's Islington-cool and far from hushed, but you could relax with anyone here – or pop in just for a pint of their handpumped ale. A treasure.

directions	Nearest tubes: Highbury & Islington; Essex Road.
meals	12pm–2.30pm (3.30pm weekends); 5.30pm–10.30pm (6.30pm Saturdays; 9.30pm Sundays). Main courses £9.50–£22.50; set menu £12.95 & £14.95.
closed	Monday lunchtimes.

directions	Nearest tubes: Angel; Highbury & Islington.
meals	Pre-theatre set menu £14.

Dan Crawford
The King's Head Theatre Pub,
115 Upper Street,
Islington, London N1 1QN
tel   020 7226 0364
web   www.kingsheadtheatre.org

Barnaby Meredith
The House,
63–69 Canonbury Road,
Islington, London N1 2DG
tel   020 7704 7410
web   www.inthehouse.biz

Map: 2 Entry: 143

Map: 2 Entry: 144

Duke of Cambridge

Geetie Singh and Esther Boulton are on a mission to raise people's awareness of food and where it comes from. At the Duke, the first of two all-organic London pubs run by Singhboulton, 'organic' and 'sustainable' are the watchwords: everything – wines, beers, spirits – is certified organic and they buy as locally as they can to cut down on food miles. Most of the beers are brewed in nearby Shoreditch, meat comes from a single farm, fish is purchased from sustainable sources. If you think it all sounds a touch worthy, this is not a meeting place for the saintlier-than-thou but a proper pub with a reputation for terrific food, drink, service and atmosphere. Heavens, you can even smoke in the bar! It's a large, airy space with a comfortable, easy, shoestring minimalism; take your fill of the eclectic, mediterranean-influenced food in here or in the big non-smoking restaurant at the back. A great place of taste and intelligence.

Dartmouth Arms

The pub has style *and* a sense of humour. Sitting unobtrusively in a Highgate side street, the Dartmouth Arms looks smart but unexceptional. Inside is another story. There's huge personality and the predominant theme is copper. It comes highly burnished, whether as water pipes, bar top or mirror frame. In the back room there's bold kitsch in a copper statue, fish in a TV-set tank and champagne bottles hanging from a chandelier. Furnishings are chic: a pine bar, black padded chairs, half-panelled walls painted vibrant red. Landlord Nick is passionate about food and beer. There are three perfectly kept cask ales, 10 wines by the glass and a modern British menu displayed on the inevitable copper boards. There's food for everyone: roast vegetable and goat's cheese tart, leek and Caerphilly sausages with tomato sauce and mash, pan-fried organic salmon. The background music is noisy at times and the pub attracts a lively crowd.

| directions | Nearest tubes: Angel & Farringdon. |
| meals | 12.30pm-3pm (3.30pm weekends); 6.30pm-10.30pm (10pm Sundays). Main courses £9.50-£16. |

Miss Geetie Singh
Duke of Cambridge,
30 St Peter's Street,
Islington, London N1 8JT

| tel | 020 7359 3066 |
| web | www.singhboulton.co.uk |

| directions | Nearest tube: Tufnell Park. |
| meals | 11am-10pm (10am Sundays). Main courses from £7. |

Nick May
Dartmouth Arms,
35 York Rise,
Dartmouth Park, London NW5 1SP

| tel | 020 7485 3267 |

Map: 2   Entry: 145

Map: 2   Entry: 146

The Junction Tavern

From the stainless-steel, open-to-view kitchen flows food that is modern European and wide-ranging – from good old Sunday roast beef to poached langoustine with new potatoes and lemon butter and a perfect fruit crumble. The daily menu is market-based and well-priced, particularly at weekday lunchtimes when main courses are pleasingly affordable. Word has spread: at weekends you book; the place heaves. Young staff are friendly and – given that this is a 'chilled' place – cheerfully attitude-free. The interior is high-ceilinged, corniced, wood-panelled, with big leather sofas and an open fire. While half the pub is restaurant, the rest is old-fashioned bar, serving beers and good wines. Enjoy a fresh glass of manzanilla in the garden in summer (or in winter, thanks to the heaters), or in the conservatory in spring. Jacky Kitching and partner Chris Leach have a background in restaurants; they also own The Northgate in Islington. This is their second gastropub.

directions	Nearest tubes: Kentish Town; Tufnell Pk.
meals	12pm-3pm (4pm weekends); 6.30pm-10.30pm (9.30pm Sundays).
	Main courses £6.50-£13.50.
closed	Xmas Eve & Day & New Year's Day.

Jacky Kitching
The Junction Tavern,
101 Fortess Road,
Kentish Town, London NW5 1AG
tel   020 7485 9400

Map: 2 Entry: 147

Ye Olde White Bear

Hampstead has jealously guarded its reputation as a village near London rather than as part of the sprawling suburbs; when you visit Ye Olde White Bear you feel it has succeeded in staving off the city's advances. There is still a villagey air to Hampstead, though there would no doubt be an outcry if anyone drove a herd of cows through the streets (there certainly was when McDonalds set up shop.) The Bear resembles a country pub on the outside and is marvellously quiet, buried down a backstreet, protected from the buses and bustle of the Heath Road. Inside, a higgledy-piggledy, reassuringly cosy local – with dark walls, a real fire, comfortable chairs. Friendly staff serve you a well-kept pint of bitter or a glass of one of their many wines, and, should you have built up an appetite by walking across that magnificent heath, there's a whole menu of nourishing pub grub – snacks, salads, sirloin steak – at reasonable (London) pub prices.

directions	Nearest tube: Hampstead.
meals	12pm-9pm.
	Main courses £7-£10.

Chris Ely
Ye Olde White Bear,
Well Road,
Hampstead, London NW3 1LJ
tel   020 7435 3758

Map: 1 Entry: 148

The Belsize

Belsize Park was once a slightly down-at-heel relation sandwiched between affluent neighbours, but, like almost every other building in the area, the exterior of the Belsize has had a fashionable lick of pastel paint. It used to be an ordinary boozer; today it is a chic and baroque dining pub with a cocktail list and its own bread oven. Yet owners Randall and Aubyn, who also own The Ifield, have cleverly managed to hold on to the old pubby feel. Enter an open bar area with a raffish mix-and-match décor that caters for a North London crowd: chandeliers hang from ceilings, gilt-framed mirrors cover the walls. There's rap and reggae and an almost louche feel, themed nights, exotic cocktails and oceans of bottled beer. Menus change regularly and are modern British in style, with prices to reflect the area. Typical dishes might include linguini and clams with chilli, lemon and parsley and crispy aromatic duck with herb and beanshoot salad. There's also a room at the back that can be hired for private parties.

directions	Nearest tube: Belsize Park.
meals	12pm-10.30pm.
	Main courses £4-£13.50.

Sam Freeman
The Belsize,
29 Belsize Lane,
Belsize Park, London NW3 5AS
tel   020 7794 4910

The Lansdowne

Abuzz with music and conversation, the Lansdowne is worth crossing several postcodes for. Amanda Pritchett was one of the founders of the trail-blazing Eagle; eight years ago she set up the Lansdowne and followed a similar gastropub route. It's laid-back, open-plan and atmospherically lit, with big wooden tables and dark green tiles – and manages, at least downstairs, to keep its pubby feel, in spite of the emphasis on dining. Upstairs is an elegant and charming 60-seat restaurant where customers are treated to adventurous food – Jerusalem artichoke and red onion risotto, sea bass en papillotte, belly of pork with mash and shallots. Though the serious dining goes on up here, you can also eat down where the decibels are high, the atmosphere shambolic and everyone loves the pizzas (kids included). There are two draught ales and one real cider, but really this is a wine and lager place. Outside in summer is a little oasis to which you can retreat and leave the city behind.

directions	Nearest tube: Chalk Farm.
meals	12pm-3pm; 7pm-10pm.
	Main courses £8-£15.
closed	Monday lunchtimes.

Amanda Pritchett
The Lansdowne,
90 Gloucester Avenue,
Primrose Hill, London NW1 8HX
tel   020 7483 0409

The Engineer

Victorian superstar Isambard Kingdom Brunel, whose silhouette decks the sign, once had an office here. Artists are the new stars and today the place is run by a painter and an actress. Behind the half-stuccoed 1850 edifice lies a cheerful, friendly gastropub with a smart bohemian feel and an outstanding reputation for food. It is particularly strong on fish cooked with a touch of the mediterranean or Pacific Rim – chargrilled squid with green papaya, say – but there are roast rack of lamb, fat homemade chips and creamy and chocolately desserts to swoon over too. Wines look to the New World and beer is excellent. Eat up or down: the front bar is relaxed, bright and buzzing, the restaurant up has white plates on white cloths, mirrors in gilt frames and art for sale. In summer, the large lush garden catches the sun and seats up to 80. There's a good mixed crowd here though the majority are hip and young. The service is often praised, and the parking is easy.

directions	Nearest tube: Camden Town.
meals	12pm-3pm; 12.30pm-3.30pm weekends; 7pm-10.30pm. Main courses £9.75-£16.

	Karen Northcote
	The Engineer,
	65 Gloucester Avenue,
	Primrose Hill, London NW1 8JH
tel	020 7722 0950
web	www.the-engineer.com

Map: 1 Entry: 151

The Crown & Goose

From the outside it looks like a twee tearoom; inside it feels like a house occupied by friendly squatters. You might wonder where the border lies between bohemian and unkempt and some would argue that this popular little pub lies on the wrong side. However, the laid-back inhabitants of Camden (where Dickens had Bob Cratchit live) don't mind a bit... people are as happy here browsing the papers as gossiping with friends. There's one big room with an elaborate wooden bar and a vaguely Victorian mishmash of tables, sofas and chairs, an open fire and music in the background. Walls are largely bare but carry the odd piece of art; look out for an unusual bronze. Service is exuberant and warm, the beer plentiful and well-priced, the food simple modern British. Typical dishes are wild-boar sausages with roasted vegetables and beetroot and apple relish; and Cuban burgers with jalapeno salad. Some say the chips are the best in town.

directions	Nearest tube: Camden Town.
meals	12pm-3pm; 6pm-10pm; 12pm-10pm Fridays & Saturdays (9pm Sundays). Main courses £8-£10.

	Joe Lowry
	The Crown & Goose,
	100 Arlington Road,
	Camden, London NW1 7HP
tel	020 7485 8008

Map: 2 Entry: 152

The Eagle

Still mighty, after all these years. The Eagle is the standard bearer of the new wave that saw off scampi-in-a-basket and similar horrors. No tablecloths, no reservations – just delicious food ordered from the bar. With its real ales and decent choice of wines, the appeal is as much for drinkers as for diners and at peak times it heaves. The atmosphere is louche and bohemian; no surprise, maybe, that the offices of the *Guardian* are next door. In spite of the laid-back appeal of scuffed floors, worn leather chairs, mix-and-match crockery, background Latin music and art gallery upstairs, the Eagle's reputation rests firmly on its food. The long bar counter is dominated by a stainless steel area at which ravishingly beautiful squid, pancetta and Mediterranean vegetables are prepared. Pasta, risotto, peasant soups, spicy steak sandwiches... it's worth the trek to get here. And how many gastropubs have a best-selling cookery book to their name?

Black Friar

Across the Thames from the Tate Modern, the only Art Nouveau pub in London – perhaps the world. It was built in 1905 and the fact that it exists today is almost entirely due to Sir John Betjeman and his noble Sixties' campaign to save it from demolition. The building's amazing wedge shape is an echo of those narrow medieval streets, long since replaced by broad thoroughfares. It stands, soaked in history, on the site not only of a Dominican Friary but also of the courthouse in which Henry VIII achieved the annulment of his marriage to Catherine of Aragon. Art Nouveau mosaics romp over walls inside and out; in the arched room off the saloon, green and red marble alabaster is embellished with cavorting friars. It can get packed at lunchtimes and evenings so go off-peak if you can. No piped music, no plush – just bare boards, unpretentious pub grub courtesy of Mitchells & Butler and good solid ales from Adnams and Tetley. But it's the architecture that's the real star here – there is no other like it.

directions	Nearest tube: Farringdon Road.
meals	12.30pm-3pm (3.30pm weekends); 6.30pm-10.30pm. Main courses £8-£12.
closed	Sunday evenings.

directions	Nearest tube/rail: Blackfriars.
meals	11am-9pm. Main courses £5-£7.50.

Michael Belben
The Eagle,
159 Farringdon Road,
Farringdon, London EC1R 3AL
tel 020 7837 1353

David Tate
Black Friar,
174 Queen Victoria Street,
Blackfriars, London EC4V 4EG
tel 020 7236 5474

Map: 2 Entry: 153

Map: 2 Entry: 154

Jerusalem Tavern

There's so much atmosphere here you could bottle it up and take it home – along with one of the beers. Old Clerkenwell – once a haunt of the Knights Templar – has reinvented itself; the quaint 1720 tavern, a former coffee house, epitomizes all that is best about the place. Its name is new, acquired seven years ago when the exemplary St Peter's Brewery of Suffolk took it over and stocked it with their ales and fruit beers. Step in to a reincarnation of a nooked and crannied interior, all bare boards and plain tables, candlelit at night with a winter fire; arrive early to bag the table on the 'gallery'. Lunchtime food is simple and English – bangers and mash, a roast, a fine platter of cheese – with ingredients coming daily from Smithfield Market down the road. There's a good selection of wines by the glass but this is a drinker's pub: staff are friendly and know their beer, and the full, irresistible range of St Peter's ales is all there, from the cask or the specially designed bottle.

directions	Nearest tube: Farringdon Road.
meals	12pm-2.30pm.
	Main courses £6-£8.
closed	Saturdays; Sundays; Bank Holidays.

John Murphy
Jerusalem Tavern,
55 Britton Street,
Clerkenwell, London EC1M 5NA
tel 020 7490 4281
web www.stpetersbrewery.co.uk

Map: 2 Entry: 155

The Peasant

A huge, nicely old-fashioned 19th-century pub with a fireplace in the corner, a massive, dark wooden bar and acres of ceiling. Over five years the Wright brothers built up a reputation for good wine, beer, cocktails and food. Now they have improved what was already a slick and sophisticated set-up, and brought in new blood to spice up the menus. Expect the freshest ingredients and quite a few surprises: grilled kangaroo with globe artichoke stuffed with shiitake mushrooms and peanuts; roast cod on fennel; edamame (soybean) and saffron broth with pickled cucumber. Mezze are served downstairs throughout the day – marinated olives and peppers, good cold meats, decent bread. The restaurant, too, has had a shake-up: a light, polished, first-floor room with a painted corner bar and a conservatory with a balcony attached. It's brilliantly positioned for antique shops, markets and visiting the Design Centre or Sadler's Wells.

directions	Nearest tube: Angel.
meals	12pm-3pm (4pm Sundays); 6pm-11pm.
	Main courses £6-£13. Mezze £3-£4.50.
closed	Saturday lunchtimes.

Gregory & Patrick Wright
The Peasant,
240 St John Street,
Islington, London EC1V 4PH
tel 020 7336 7726
web www.thepeasant.co.uk

Map: 2 Entry: 156

The White Swan

It had spent the previous 20 years as the Mucky Duck – and had become, of late, very mucky indeed. Now it's a cool, new swan. At plain tables on fashionably unpolished boards, City traders quaff real ales (there are four) and fine wines (20 by the glass). Upstairs is a mezzanine level, a stylish banquette-seated restaurant with a mirrored ceiling and some unusually good cooking. Dishes are an enticing, flavoursome mix of robust (rump of lamb with crushed olive-oil potato and salad niçoise) and subtle (fricassée of monkfish with fennel, chervil and truffle oil). Cheese and wine lists are encyclopaedic, vegetables and side dishes expensively 'extra'. Uniquely, they have lockers for regular customers in which to store a bottle of unfinished wine. The bar menu veers from sourdough sandwiches to dishes that change with seasons… with a bit of luck you'll find seared rabbit with roast tomatoes, chorizo, basil and crème fraîche on yours. The accompanying homemade foccacia is wonderful.

directions	Nearest tube: Chancery Lane.
meals	12pm-3pm; 6pm-10.00pm.
	Main courses (bar) £9; set menus £18-£22.
closed	Weekends; 3pm-6pm.

Tom & Ed Martin
The White Swan,
108 Fetter Lane,
Holborn, London EC4A 1ES
tel   020 7242 9696
web   www.thewhiteswanlondon.com

Map: 2 Entry: 157

Old Bank of England

The solid Italianite exterior prepares you for the splendour within. It was built in 1888 as the Law Courts' branch of the Bank of England and it remained a bank right up until 1994. Then Fuller's Brewery, with help from the Heritage Committee, transformed it into a lavish pie-and-ale house. In the First World War the Crown Jewels were kept in steel-lined vaults downstairs – these now house the kitchens – while the two bars are linked by a magnificent stair. High ceilings are elaborately moulded, there are marble pillars, grand murals, glittering chandeliers. No. 194's other claim to fame is that it is on the site of a certain Mrs Lovett's pie shop. Mrs Lovett was the partner-in-crime of the demon barber, Sweeney Todd, who reputedly dug a tunnel from his shop 200 yards down Fleet Street along which he dragged his victims for use in Mrs Lovett's pies. Today's pies are less challenging – basic pub grub, in fact – while the beers are Fuller's best, and there's a long wine list.

directions	Nearest tube: Fleet Street.
meals	12pm-9pm.
	Main courses £7-£10.

Mark Maltby
Old Bank of England,
194 Fleet Street,
Holborn, London EC4A 2LT
tel   020 7430 2255
web   www.fullers.co.uk

Map: 2 Entry: 158

The Seven Stars

Nudging the backdoor of the Royal Courts of Justice, the Seven Stars is primarily a barristers' and litigants' den. Here since 1602, it was originally the haunt of Dutch sailors, and named after the seven provinces of the Netherlands. Having survived the Great Fire by a whisker it's been here longer than the courts themselves. Until recently it was looking tired, even exhausted; in the last three years it has been transformed by the exotically named Roxy Beaujolais, landlady and head chef. The glorious single bar has hung on to its boarded floors, low beams, old mirrors and narrow wood settles, and framed vintage legal film posters line the red walls. In 2003 the utterly old-fashioned, unspoilt and diminutive Seven Stars won the *Time Out* London Pub of the Year award, and has been dubbed "near-perfect". The menu is short and bistro-like: roast chicken and aioli, rib-eye steak sandwich, a plate of charcuterie. Harveys bitters are the house beers and there is a very decent selection of wines.

directions	Nearest tubes: Chancery Lane & Temple.
meals	12pm–3pm; 6pm–9pm. Main courses £6.50–£9.50.
closed	Sundays.

Roxy Beaujolais
The Seven Stars,
53 Carey Street,
Holborn, London WC2A 2JB
tel   020 7242 8521

Map: 2 Entry: 159

French House

This is something of an exception. As the French House does not serve pumped ale, it would not, by some lights, qualify as a pub – but no guide to British inns and public houses would be complete without it. The legendary Soho haunt, once patronised by members of the French Resistance, has been – and still is – befriended by famous Londoners (Freud, Melly), international figureheads and a welter of journalists, writers and bohemians who spend their days and nights in Soho. Dylan Thomas lost the only manuscript of *Under Milk Wood* here while on a bender. Despite the gentrification of Soho and the pub's renown, 'The French' has a delightfully scuffed-around-the-edges feel and attracts a friendly, bacchanalian crowd from many walks of life. There's bar food in the small, packed, smoky bar, and a cosy, funky restaurant upstairs with a late license. But this is first and foremost a drinking den (half pints of John Smith's, Beamish, Guinness) and a vastly atmospheric one at that.

directions	Nearest tube: Leicester Square.
meals	12pm–3pm; 6pm–11pm. No food Sundays. Main courses £2.50–£5.

Noel Botham
French House,
49 Dean Street,
Soho, London W1D 5BG
tel   020 7437 2477

Map: 2 Entry: 160

Windsor Castle

One of the joys of exploring London is that sometimes you chance upon an unexpected find – like the Windsor Castle, an extraordinary distillation of 20th-century pubbery in a quiet backwater off the Edgware Road, guarded by a model soldier. Run for 16 years by Michael Tierney, who was a publican in Marylebone for several more, it brims with plaques, coins, statues, signed photos of patrons (Peter O'Toole, George Best) and, above all, royal and Sir Winston Churchill memorabilia. (Republicans are welcome.) You'd be forgiven for thinking it was an antique shop. It is, however, an extremely friendly pub. Known as 'God's Waiting Room' – its clientele not being in the first flush of youth – it is also the monthly meeting place of that great British institution, the Handlebar Moustache Society, whose magnificent achievements are photographically illustrated by the entrance. Decent Thai food is served in the bar and in the wee, warm restaurant upstairs.

directions	Nearest tube: Edgware Road.
meals	12pm-3pm; 6pm-10pm. No food Saturday lunchtimes. Main courses £5.95-8.95.

	Michael Tierney
	Windsor Castle,
	29 Crawford Place,
	Marylebone, London W1H 4LJ
tel	020 7723 4371

Map: 1 Entry: 161

The Grenadier

Down a cobbled alley on the Grosvenor estate, the tiny Grenadier is unmissable, with its fanfare of patriotic paintwork, tumbling flowers and red sentry box. It is a magnet for tourists and their cameras. Small, uneven steps lead to a cosy interior with a military theme – a reflection of this little watering hole's glorious past. Originally the Duke of Wellington's officers' mess, it later became a popular place for King George IV to enjoy a pint, then was frequented by Madonna. The dimly lit Mess Bar, with smouldering coal fire, is stuffed with memorabilia: gleaming breast plates, swords, bearskins and bugles. Behind, in the small restaurant, squeeze in and settle down to beef Wellington or fish and chips at battle-themed bench seats and tables dressed in starched white linen. In September, the ghost of an officer – accidentally flogged to death after cheating at cards – returns to haunt the place, while the infamous Bloody Marys are best sampled on Sundays, from a specially erected bar. A small place with a big heart.

directions	Nearest tube: Hyde Park Corner.
meals	12pm-1.30pm (3pm Sundays); 6pm-9pm. Main courses £5-£8.50.

	Mr Cellan Williams
	The Grenadier,
	18 Wilton Row,
	Belgravia, London SW1X 7NR
tel	020 7235 3074
web	www.thespiritgroup.com

Map: 1 Entry: 162

Nags Head

Once known as the smallest pub in London, the Nags Head expanded in Victorian times, but modestly; it could still lay claim to its title today. This wooden-floored and panelled boozer may be small but it has huge personality. The tiny bar is low enough to serve passing gnomes, hence the sunken floor behind, allowing bar staff to meet seated drinkers eye to eye. Walls and ceilings are packed with interesting memorabilia, including a squadron of nicotine-stained matchstick bi-planes and a 'What the Butler Saw' machine – operational in exchange for a donation to the pub's charity pot. No fruit machines, no mobile phones, but music hall songs from the 20s and 30s, open fires and loads of nostalgia; it's a great little place to quaff Adnams ales or a glass of Aspall's Suffolk cider. Downstairs, on checked cloths, a great spread of home-cooked meats, pies, cheeses and salads can be scoffed at lunchtime, along with other hot 'Kitchen Favourites', like real ale sausages.

directions	Nearest tube: Hyde Park Corner.
meals	11am-9.30pm.
	Main courses £6.50-£10.50.

Kevin Moran
Nags Head,
53 Kinnerton Street,
Knightsbridge, London SW1X 8ED
tel   020 7235 1135

Swag & Tails

Hidden down a pretty mews in one of the most fashionable parts of town, the little whitewashed pub with blue shutters and well-clipped topiary is an easy walk – even in Jimmy Choos – from the main Harvey Nichols-Harrods drag. Escape the crowds and rest weary feet in the warm, yellow-and-blue interior where wooden floors and swagged curtains make a fresh and glamorous alternative to the heavy trimmings of the traditional Knightsbridge pub. The attractive tiled conservatory at the back – less noisy and smoky than the main bar – is a delightful spot in which to tuck into seared king scallops with lemon dill sauce or chargrilled lamb chops, couscous and herbed yogurt. The food is stylish, modern and really very good. Staff are full of smiles and, if it takes an explorer to find this little place, the wonderful black and white photograph of Nare's Arctic expedition of 1875 – a present from landlady Annemaria to her husband – is a fitting first reward for your perseverance.

directions	2 minutes walk from Harrods.
meals	12pm-3pm; 6pm-10pm.
	Main courses £7.50-£13.25.
closed	Weekends; Bank Holidays.

Ms Annemaria Boomer-Davies
Swag & Tails,
10-11 Fairholt Street,
Knightsbridge, London SW7 1EG
tel   020 7584 6926
web   www.swagandtails.com

Map: 1 Entry: 163

Map: 4 Entry: 164

Coopers Arms

A refreshing pit-stop not far from the glitzy King's Road – you'd be forgiven for thinking you'd stepped into the 1930s, and a station waiting room at that. Find wooden floors, dark furniture, high ceilings, cream and burgundy paintwork, old railway posters on the walls. Yet there's a contemporary feel to it all and the space is big, airy and light. Head to the bar for Young's Bitter and Special, Smiles' IPA or some wholesome pub food. The homemade lamb burgers, with ingredients fresh from proprietor Charles Gotto's organic farm, are a big hit, along with roast pimento and tomato soup and traditional temptations like apple and berry crumble and custard. Upstairs, a newly done-up function room with long trestle table; downstairs, a stuffed brown bear, a mounted moose head and organic eggs for sale. This is an uncomplicated, down-to-earth pub with some fun and original touches – you could happily stay for a pint or two on a Sunday with the papers.

Builders Arms

You wouldn't expect such an exquisite little pub in the back streets of the King's Road. Enter and be seduced: the country-living-room feel is so comforting you might want to move in. Pints of London Pride are downed among large puffy armchairs, low table lamps, walls in soft greens and creams, and in a ruby-red snug behind the bar. 'Never trust a builder without a tattoo' reads the sign on the wall, but the people here, and their pooches, are as immaculate as the interior. This popular watering hole draws a lively mix of locals, business folk and shoppers. The Builders is a stylish pub, even if labelling the loos 'Builders' and 'Ballerinas' is a touch twee, and the food is modern British attractively presented: smoked haddock, saffron and spring onion risotto, grilled rib-eye steak with garlic and parsley butter. Avoid Friday lunchtimes: they're packed.

directions	Nearest tube: Sloane Square.
meals	12.30pm-3pm; 6.30pm-9.30pm. No food Sunday evenings. Main courses £7.50-£12.

directions	Nearest tubes: Sloane Street & South Kensington. Behind King's Road, between Sydney Street & Chelsea Green.
meals	12pm-3pm; 7pm-9.45pm. Main courses £8.95-£13.95.

	Charles Gotto
	Coopers Arms,
	87 Flood Street,
	Chelsea, London SW3 5TB
tel	020 7376 3120
web	www.thecoopers.co.uk

	Rupert Clevely
	Builders Arms,
	13 Britten Street,
	Chelsea, London SW3 3TY
tel	020 7349 9040
web	www.geronimo-inns.co.uk

Map: 4 Entry: 165

Map: 4 Entry: 166

The Atlas

Up high, golden letters on wooden panelling proclaim London Stout, Burton Bitter and mild ales. The Atlas is a great little place in which to delve into more modern brews: Fuller's London Pride, Caledonian Deuchars IPA, Adnams Broadside. A glazed wooden partition – a prop for the 'Wine of the Moment' blackboard – divides the bar in two. Other Thirties' features remain: floorboards, attractive black and white tiling around the foot of the bar and three brick fireplaces, two of which add a glow in winter. The third, its mantelpiece piled high with lemons and limes, has been converted into a serving hatch for mediterranean-inspired dishes – grilled sardines, Italian sausages, Spanish sliced meats; the wine list trumpets 24 wines by the glass. Doors lead to a walled suntrap garden (open from May till October) where puffa-jacketed Fulhamites flock under the rain and wind cover. In spite of its modest frontage on a residential street, the pub is next to a big Pay & Display, so not hard to find.

| directions | Nearest tube: West Brompton. |
| meals | 12.30pm-3pm; 7pm-10.30pm (10pm Sundays). Main courses £6.50-£12. |

George Manners
The Atlas,
16 Seagrave Road,
Fulham, London SW6 1RX
tel   020 7385 9129

Map: 4 Entry: 167

Chelsea Ram

A quiet residential street off the Lots Road seems an unlikely place to find a corner pub bursting with bonhomie. It used to be a junk shop; now the fine arched shop windows with etched glass are complemented by soft and subtle mustards and terracottas, tongue-and-groove cladding, a dark green wooden bar and colourful local art. A carpeted area to the back, with its small alcoves, soft lighting and shelves of thumbed books, is an intimate spot in which to be treated to some enticing, Roux-inspired food: smoked haddock and spinach perhaps ("posh fish pie"), followed by chocolate pudding with Baileys sauce. The scrubbed wooden tables are a great place for lively card games (please bring your own) over coffee. Close to the large storage depot of Bonhams the auctioneers, this popular pub has done well for itself and is worth the few minutes' walk from the end of the King's Road.

| directions | Nearest tube: Fulham Broadway; Sloane Square. |
| meals | 12pm-10pm (9.30pm Sundays). Main courses £3.95-£11.95. |

Jeremy Lee
Chelsea Ram,
32 Burnaby Street,
Chelsea, London SW10 0PL
tel   020 7351 4008

Map: 4 Entry: 168

Harwood Arms

Of all of the gastropubs in Rupert Clevely's impressive chain, the Harwood Arms stands out. Unusual, too, to find a pub so close to Chelsea football ground that dares depart from the strictly traditional. There's an unashamedly contemporary feel here, and Rupert flaunts his love of Africa: wonderful earthy colours – reds, oranges, aubergines, browns and creams – wooden floors and a slightly more formal dining area with seagrass woven in deep colours creates the perfect backdrop for exotic *objets d'art*. Texture is king – huge feather-filled velvet cushions, some bright orange tribal hats, a striking canvas of thick bright oils, a row of black and white African portraits in wide wooden frames. The Harwood encourages an easy informality where, over a pint of Youngs or Spitfire, you dine on good modern dishes, cut your own bread (homemade, of course) and help yourself to oils and vinegar from a long central table.

directions	Nearest tube: Fulham Broadway. Pub to east of North End Road on corner of Welham Grove & Farm Lane.
meals	12pm-2.45pm (4pm Sundays); 7pm-9.45pm (9.30pm Sundays). Main courses £5.95-£10.50.

	Ben Hurley
	Harwood Arms,
	29 Walham Grove,
	Fulham, London SW6 1QR
tel	020 7386 1847
web	www.geronimo-inns.co.uk

Map: 4 Entry: 169

White Horse

The pub on the green is reputed to have the best-kept beers in Europe. Mark Dorber's remarkable knowledge of real ale is the fruit of years working with the best tasters and encouragement from good trade journalists. His place is a shrine, his glorious two-day beer festival in November brings buffs from far and wide to consume 300 British ales, and the ever-changing list of guest ales above the log fire is within reading distance of some deeply comfortable sofas. Bar food is of the best sort, from ploughman's with unusual cheeses to fried bass with garlic mash, and the menu usefully suggests the best accompanying liquor. Inside, terracotta walls, slatted wooden blinds, lovingly polished pumps and beer memorabilia; outside, a big terrace overlooking the green and a Sunday barbecue. The pub may be a hotbed of Fulhamites, but whoever dubbed it 'The Sloaney Pony' was misguided; given such a passion for beer, 'The Frisky Fermenting Filly' might seem more appropriate.

directions	Nearest tube: Parsons Green.
meals	12pm-3.30pm; 6pm-10.30pm; 12pm-10.30pm weekends. Main courses £7.75-£13.95.

	Mark Dorber
	White Horse,
	1 Parsons Green,
	Fulham, London SW6 4UL
tel	020 7736 2115
web	www.whitehorsesw6.com

Map: 4 Entry: 170

The Scarsdale

We can only be grateful to the French builder who believed Napoleon would invade and built The Scarsdale as living quarters for the French army. The immaculate Edwardes Square could only have been built by the French. This is a delightful little pub with a summer terrace of hanging baskets and bags of Victorian character. The old stained glass, dark panelling and burgundy walls provide a distinguished foil for old paintings in heavily gilded frames and various empty magnums of champagne, while the happy hum of quaffers flows from cosy corners as easily as the ales. Fabulous smells emanate from the kitchen hatch heralding the arrival of slow-roasted lamb shoulder with haricots blancs and minted gravy, expertly followed by hot chocolate pudding. Eat in the busy bar or in the swagged dining room. You could happily go on a first date here, or bring the parents.

directions	Nearest tube: High Street Kensington.
meals	12pm-10pm (9pm Sundays). Main courses £8-£14.
closed	Christmas Day.

Roy & Sarah Dodgeson
The Scarsdale,
23a Edwardes Square,
Kensington, London W8 6HE
tel   020 7937 1811

Map: 4 Entry: 171

Churchill Arms

It's hard to say which comes first in the popularity stakes, the publican or the pub: Gerry O'Brien is an influential figure and this is a terrific pub. The Churchill is not only a shrine to the great prime minster but to Gerry's collections of memorabilia and his irrepressible Irish humour. To the left of the counter in the bar – smoky, cosy with open fire – is Chamber Lane (115 chamber pots suspended from the ceiling that Gerry is "potty about") while the walls of the leafy, glass-roofed Thai restaurant – once, unbelievably, a garage – display his prized butterflies. Never mind the tourists; come for great Guinness and beers, oriental feasts that don't break the bank, bags of atmosphere and a big dollop of tradition. On the annual celebration of Sir Winston's birthday unsuspecting drinkers are amazed to see everyone dressed in 40s style; sausage and mash can be bought for a shilling and the evening's takings go to the Cabinet War Office Museum. You have been warned!

directions	Nearest tube: High Street Kensington.
meals	12pm-9.30pm. Main courses £5.85.

Gerry O'Brian
Churchill Arms,
119 Kensington Church Street,
Kensington, London W8 7LN
tel   020 7727 4242

Map: 1 Entry: 172

Ladbroke Arms

The warm glow emanating from the sage-painted sash windows is enough to tempt anyone into the Ladbroke Arms. Cream-painted and ginger hessian walls, benches plump with autumnal-hued cushions, long shiny tables, paintings, books... and beers to please real enthusiasts: Fuller's London Pride, Greene King IPA and Abbot Ale, Adnams Bitter. The intimate Ladbroke takes its food seriously, too, the chef buying cheese twice weekly from a touring supplier and placing orders with a fishing fleet every day. The bar is adorned with a sparkling collection of olive oils, vinegars and bottled fruit; in the raised restaurant area foodies tuck into intensely flavoured dishes such as aubergine, tomato and taleggio tart, sea bass with squid and risotto nero and braised lamb faggots with rosemary jus. Sunday roasts are a favourite among well-heeled locals; the hot chocolate fondant pudding is legendary. Sup under the parasols in summer as Notting Hillbillies smooch by.

directions	Nearest tubes: Notting Hill Gate & Holland Park.
meals	12pm-2.30pm (3pm weekends). Main courses £9.50-£14.50.

J Shubrati
Ladbroke Arms,
54 Ladbroke Road,
Holland Park, London W11 3NW
tel 020 7727 6648
web www.capitalpubcompany.co.uk

The Westbourne

Come to see and be seen! Danny Boyle and Olly Daniaud took the place on a few years ago and gave it a thorough going over. Westbourne Park Villas promptly became the trendiest place in England and it's worth arriving early... 11am perhaps. London's beau monde amasses throughout the day at this shabby-chic gastropub, keen to spend gaily for decent beers and scrummy food. In the main bars is a collection of old tables and chairs, with some lush sofas at the back; walls spill over, bistro-style, with posters, photos and original art. The terrace at the front with its gas heaters is an all-year drinking spot – and just about handles the overflow. Chef Neil Parfitt's style is robust modern British and the ingredients he uses are the freshest: oysters, salmon, grilled fish, pan-fried duck breast with juniper jus, chargrilled venison steak with braised red cabbage. But most are here for the scene as much as the food.

directions	Nearest tube: Westbourne Park.
meals	12.30pm-3pm (3.30pm weekends); 7pm-10pm (9.30pm Friday-Sunday). Main courses £8-£12.50.
closed	Monday lunchtimes.

Wood Davis
The Westbourne,
101 Westbourne Park Villas,
London W2 5ED
tel 020 7221 1332
web www.thewestbourne.com

Map: 1 Entry: 173

Map: 1 Entry: 174

West

Paradise by Way of Kensal Green

The exotic name was poached from G K Chesterton. Locals may have been taken aback when the bohemian bar first opened; now the area is full of the young and fashionable who little realise that The Paradise – all fairy lights and candles, background jazz and blues – stands on the site of the oldest pub in Brent. A statue of a fallen angel on the wall stares down in surprise on the battered reproduction Regency sofas, wrought-iron garden tables and chairs, and vast palm fronds growing in even vaster planters. The bar itself is small and not the most comfortable but there's still a pubby feel. The place isn't too self-obsessed (in spite of the odd C-list celebrity) and nor are the people who come here. Pop in for a pint of real ale and to look at the papers, or stay for a meal (must book). The menu is modern European with an oriental twist and the food extremely good: Thai green curry, penne with grilled aubergine, artichoke hearts, tomatoes and black olives, beef fillet with peppercorn sauce.

directions	Nearest tube: Kensal Green.
meals	12.30pm-4pm; 7pm-11pm (12.30pm-9pm Sundays). Main courses £8-£9; set menu £10.

Linda McConnell & Paul Halpin
Paradise by Way of Kensal Green,
19 Kilburn Lane,
Kensal Rise, London NW10 4AE
tel   020 8969 0098

Map: 1 Entry: 175

South

Earl Spencer

The main drag of Merton Road is not where you expect to find a pub run with passion. But the grand old Earl Spencer's spit 'n' sawdust days are over, its fine Edwardian interior stylishly restored. Now, to a clean backdrop of deep cream and dark blue, gilded ceiling mouldings and a winter fire, you will discover some of the best pub food in south London. Chef Mark Robinson and his team bake bread twice a day, have a smokery on the premises and a collection of cookery books to tempt you at the bar. A blackboard chalks up an ever-changing seasonal menu with inventive dishes popping up every day; perhaps fish soup with aioli and chive; pheasant, pigeon and Parma ham terrine with gooseberry chutney; poached pear, honey and brandy parfait. Jonathan Cox has not forgotton the Earl Spencer's roots, so there's a fine selection of wine (10 by the glass), ales (Hook Norton, Shepherd Neame Spitfire) and Hoegaarden on tap. A place to unwind... fresh flowers and papers, laid-back staff, happy drinkers, contented dogs.

directions	Nearest tube: Southfields.
meals	12.30pm-2.30pm (3pm Sundays); 7pm-10pm (9.30pm Sundays). Main courses £7.50-£12.

Jonathan Cox
Earl Spencer,
260-262 Merton Road,
Southfields, London SW18 5JL
tel   020 8870 9244

Map: 4 Entry: 176

The Garrison Public House

Do dinner and a movie – there's a rough-and-ready cinema downstairs with films on Sunday nights, and a great little restaurant up. Gastropub veterans Clive Watson and Adam White have taken on an old Victorian pub, kept the engraved glass windows and remodelled the rest into a light and airy, bare-boarded space. The furniture is silver-sprayed, lamps and objets fill every cranny. Fresh food, from apricots to Orkney mussels, arrives daily from the market down the road, and is reconstructed into dishes that are elaborate but not overly so. With a glass of rioja or a bottle of St Peter's, you'll polish off your roast cod with ribbon leeks and a shrimp and chive sauce in no time at all – or duck breast with shallots, thyme and fondant potato. Snacks include beans on toast. The kitchen is open, staff attractively laid-back, decibels are high, tables are crammed. The place is filled with fashionistas visiting the Fashion Museum and bounces with bonhomie. Forget hushed conversation.

Greenwich Union

Master brewer Alastair Hook has turned this Greenwich boozer into a shrine to his beers. The rich golds and browns of the interior reflect the hues of the glorious ales he painstakingly creates at the nearby Meantime Brewery; his Red, Golden, Amber and Chocolate ales slip down so easily that Sainsbury's has now made them part of their range. (If you're not sure which one to go for, helpful staff behind the bar will give you a taster.) This quirky little pub also serves some fine food, the Spanish chef willing to concoct delicious tapas at short notice. On Sundays, the so-called Potty Roasters take over the kitchen, feeding eager diners with succulent roasts, fresh vegetables and "crazy gravy". All, including children and dogs, are welcome here, and the spontaneous creativity of local residents, fuelled by Alastair's beers, is a rich source of entertainment for a lively crowd on the famous, regular Open Mike Nights.

directions	Nearest tube: London Bridge.
meals	12.30pm-3.30pm (4pm Sundays); 6.30pm-10pm (9.30pm Sundays). Main courses (bar) £8-£12.

directions	Exit Greenwich station, left & 2nd right (Royal Hill), pub on right.
meals	12.30pm-10pm (5pm weekends). Main courses £5.50-£7.50.

Clive Watson & Adam White
The Garrison Public House,
99 Bermondsey Street,
London Bridge, London SE1 0PA

| tel | 020 7089 9355 |
| web | www.thegarrison.co.uk |

Alastair Hook
Greenwich Union,
56 Royal Hill,
Greenwich, London SE10 8RT

| tel | 020 8692 6258 |
| web | www.meantimebrewing.co.uk |

Map: 2 Entry: 181

Map: 6 Entry: 182

There is only one place worth visiting in London for good, impartial tourist advice. It is the British Visitor Centre at No. 1 Lower Regent Street, London SW1 (9am-6.30pm Monday to Friday, 10am-4pm weekends: Tel: 020 8846 9000; www.visitbritain.com). Staff here are friendly, helpful, informative and give impartial advice, while the book shop has the largest collection of London guides and maps that I came across while researching this book (though the bigger London book shops should be well-stocked, too). It is run by the British Tourist Authority, a government-funded organisation, that is there to serve you, not to fleece you of your last penny; most places in London seem to have the latter in mind. The stark truth is that most tourist information centres in London, such as the London Tourist Information Centres, are nearly all privately run and they make their money by charging commission fees on the tours they sell. This doesn't mean they will charge you more, but they are always trying to 'sell'. Be careful and don't feel you have to follow their suggestions. The London Tourist Board is little better, and though it is government-funded, it spends its budget marketing London, and not on providing information to tourists free of charge in London. I spent two hours trying to speak to a human being in their employ; the only ones I could find were in the press office. Instead, you have to listen to recorded information listing hundreds of information lines, all of which cost 60p a minute to call; again, beware. I tried to speak to the Greater London Authority (GLA), London's governing body, but there was no one to take my call. So buy your guide books before you come, read them well, plan a flexible itinerary, commit the London tube map to memory and pack your walking boots. If you're staying in a B&B, ask your hosts – they're Londoners, they will know. In hotels, staff often have up-to-date information on what's good and what's not. I found the following guides all excellent: *Time Out*, *Lonely Planet* and Footprint's *London Handbook*.

Newspapers and magazines

The *Evening Standard* is London's newspaper. You can buy it anywhere from about 10.30am. Its web site is www.thisislondon.co.uk. *Metro* is a free paper that you pick up at tube stations. It has cinema listings etc, but it's popular, so pick one up early. *Time Out* is the magazine dedicated to London leisure; whatever you want, start looking here. It has listings for clubs, theatres, cinemas, lectures, concerts, sport... if it goes on in London, they list it. You can buy it anywhere or see www.timeout.com. If you want to

buy something second-hand in London, try the newspaper *Loot*. It's printed four times a week and you can track down just about anything in its pages. You'll find it in any newsagent.

Cinemas

London has some excellent cinemas. Best of the lot is the National Film Theatre (020 7928 3232), "a force of knowledge for anyone who cares about film", to quote Robert Altman. Its three screens are dedicated to world cinema and can be found at South Bank, SE1. It also hosts the London Film Festival for three weeks each November. Riverside Studios (020 8237 1111) in Crisp Road, W6 has a good programme of world cinema, both past and present, with double bills daily for only £5.50. The Odeon Leicester Square is expensive

at £9.50/£11.50 a ticket, but it has a huge screen and is the venue of most London premieres. There are about 50 cinemas in central London and its immediate fringe. *The Evening Standard* lists them all daily.

Theatres

The Donmar (020 7369 1732) in Covent Garden is the best-known venue for modern English theatre. Sam Mendes (of *American Beauty*-fame) put the place on the map with Nicole Kidman in *The Blue Room*. The Almeida (020 7359 4404) in Islington has also been in the vanguard over the last ten years. The National Theatre (020 7452 3400) at South Bank, Waterloo, is still a vital force 26 years after its creation. The Royal Shakespeare Company (RSC) remains the guardian of the old boy's work, but embraces modern stuff, too. You can see them at the Barbican (020 7638 8891), the Young Vic in Waterloo (020 7928 6363), or the Globe theatre (020 7401 9919) at Bankside between May and September (it's open air). The Royal Court (020 7565 5000) in Sloane Square also has a good reputation. All listings, including the West End, appear in *The Evening Standard* every day. To book, either contact each theatre direct or try Ticketmaster (020 7344 4444 or www.ticketmaster.co.uk.)

Museums

Public museums are once again free to enter, though you may have to pay to see certain temporary or visiting exhibitions. The Museum of London (150 London Wall EC2: 020 7600 3699) charts London's rise from prehistoric times to the present day, via the Romans, the great fire and two world wars. The Cromwell Road/Exhibition Road axis finds London's 'big three': the Natural History Museum (020 7942 5000), the Science Museum (020 7942 4455) and the Victoria and Albert (or V&A: 020 7938 8500). The British Museum (Great Russell Street, WC1: 020 7636 1555), Elgin Marbles included, is one of the great museums of the world. The Design Museum (28 Shad Thames, SE1: 020 7403 6933; admission £6) is full of cutting-edge innovation. The MCC Museum at Lord's (St John's Wood, NW8: 020 7432 1033) has everything for the cricket-obsessed, including the Ashes. The National Maritime Museum at Greenwich (SE10: 020 8858 4422; admission £7.50) has all things nautical, including the bullet that killed Nelson; you can buy a joint ticket for this and the Royal Observatory for under £9.50 and, at the later, stand on the meridian line. London is also full of small, quirky museums. A couple include: the Museum of Gardening History (Lambeth Palace Road, SE1: 020 7401 8865), the Petrie Museum of Egyptian Archaeology (University College London, Malet Place, WC1: 020 7504 2884) and Thomas Carlyle's house (24 Cheyne Row, SW3: 020 7352 7087; admission £4); Carlyle was visited here by friends such as Dickens, Thackeray, Tennyson and Ruskin. For a more detailed list check out www.artgalleries-london.com/museums.

Galleries

London is full of art galleries; again, many are free for access to collections, but charge for particular exhibitions. A selection includes: the Tate Modern (Queen's Walk, SE1: 020 7887 8000), the hottest space in town, its huge home in the old Bankside power station as impressive as its content (Picasso, Matisse, Pollock, Mondrian); its sister gallery, Tate Britain (Millbank, SW1: 020 7887 8008), is an archive of British art from 1500s onwards; the Hayward Gallery (South Bank Centre, SE1: 020 7928 3144; admission £8), is London's most popular exhibition centre for visiting contemporary shows; the National Gallery (Trafalgar Square, WC2: 020 7839 3321) has over 2,000 pictures from across the centuries and around the world; the National Portrait Gallery (St Martin's Place, WC2: 020 7306 0055) is exactly what it says: portraits of great Brits from the last 500 years or so, and now includes a video of sleeping beauty, David Beckham; the Queen's Gallery (Buckingham Gate, SW1: 020 7839 1377) gives partial access to the Royal Collection; the Royal Academy of Arts (Piccadilly, W1: 020 7300 8000; admission £7–£12) is worth a visit for the building alone – a real London gem; the Whitechapel Art Gallery (020 7522 7888) shows nothing but contemporary art, much the work of Young British Artists, as does the Saatchi Gallery (County Hall, SE1: 020 7823 2363; admission £8). For more big names try the Courtauld Collection (Somerset House, Strand, WC2: 020 7848 2526; admission £5) for Van Gogh, Renoir and Monet, or the Wallace Collection (Manchester Square, W1: 020 7935 0687) for Titian, Rembrandt and Rubens; finally, the Dulwich Picture Gallery

Picture
www.paulgroomphotography.com

(College Road, SE21: 020 8693 5254; admission £7) is the country's oldest public gallery and has a fine collection of old masters. For more listings, check www.artgalleries-london.com – an excellent, in-depth site, which also has an extensive diary page, where you can see what's on each day, week, month – invaluable information if you like that sort of thing.

Music venues
Classical
Four spring to mind, though London is good at classical music on a local level and many churches put on concerts during the year or hold weekly recitals. Of the bigger places, most famous of all is the Royal Albert Hall (Kensington Gore, SW7: 020 7589 8212), which holds its famous Proms concerts from mid-July to mid-September. You can often turn up on the night and get a ticket on the door. The hall itself is one of London's landmark buildings, with the incredibly beautiful Albert Memorial standing in the park opposite. The South Bank (SE1: 020 7960 4242) have three spaces for classical music: the Royal Festival Hall, the Queen Elizabeth Hall and the Purcell Room – London's top three, a must for classical-music lovers. The Barbican (EC2: 020 7638 8891) holds regular concerts and is the home of the London Symphony Orchestra. Wigmore Hall (36

Wigmore Street, W1: 020 7935 2141) is entirely independent and has huge variety.

Rock and Pop

Big bands love big venues in big cities and anyone who's anyone ends up in London at some time. Their concerts tend to be extremely popular, and if you try to get tickets on the day, expect to be disappointed. The Brixton Academy (211 Stockwell Road, SW9: 020 7771 3000) is one of the best places to see big acts. Earl's Court (Warwick Road, SW5: 020 7385 1200) packs 12,000 people in, often for fairly naff acts. The Hammersmith Apollo is an old favourite and gets the big names (Queen Caroline Street, W6: 0870 400 0700). The Marquee (Parkfield Street, N1: 7228 4400) has been revamped recently by Eurythmic Dave Stewart. Shepherd's Bush Empire (Shepherd's Bush Green, W6: 020 7771 2000) is one of the best places in town to see big concerts; Wembley Arena (Empire Way, Wembley: 020 8902 0902) is one of the worst, packs in 10,000 people and is a pain to get to. For something special try the 60-year-old 100 Club (100 Oxford Street, W1: 020 7636 0933), erstwhile haunt of Glenn Miller; you'll get masterful jazz and the odd indie rock band.

Acoustics, Country, Folk, Irish...

The 12 Bar Club (22-23 Denmark Place, off Denmark Street, WC2: 020 7916 6989) squeezes itself into the smallest of spaces making it London's cosiest night spot; country, folk and acoustic acts all play here. The Africa Centre (38 King Street, WC2: 020 7836 1973) is mostly limited to Friday nights, but the music is good.

Jazz

Ronnie Scotts (47 Frith Street, W1: 020 7439 0747) is London's best-known venue and all the greats come to play. It's not cheap, but very funky. The Vortex (139-141 Stoke Newington Church Street, N16: 020 7254 6516) may take some getting to, but this north London crown-jewel of jazz is outstanding; it's where the jazz community gathers, an exceptional place, so don't dawdle. The Jazz Café (5 Parkway, NW1: 020 7344 0044) is one of Camden's best-known night spots and popular, too, so book if you want to be sure. Pizza Express (10 Dean Street, W1: 020 7439 8722) puts on jazz in the basement seven days a week at 9pm. The 606 Club (90 Lots Road, SW6: 020 7352 5953) in Fulham is firmly established on the London jazz circuit, and is nightly. Finally, the Bull's Head (373 Lonsdale Road, SW13: 020 8876 5241) over in Barnes gets the nod from fanatics and has something every night, Sunday lunch, too. Nice.

Restaurants

I have mentioned restaurants in the text if I know them to be good or if they were heartily recommended by owners. London has thousands of places where you can eat, from workmen's cafes for all-day breakfasts (our real national cuisine?) to Gordon Ramsay and his Michelin stars. Food in London is expensive; the bill never seems to be less than £20 per head, often for no more than a main course and a glass or two of house wine. B&B owners and hotel staff will always be able to recommend somewhere to eat, but if you'd like a more comprehensive source, Harden's publish two excellent guides: *London Restaurants*, and *Good Cheap Eats in London*. You can get them in any London bookshop – your stomach will thank you for it if you do – or see www.hardens.com.

Cafés

Café-culture has come to London, but mainly with the big chains, and the British remain suspicious about going out at night to a place where they cannot order alcohol. A shame; it would be good to see a return to the coffee houses of the 18th century that "distinguished London from all other cities." There were over 2,000 of them in the early 1700s. A few exceptional places can be found. Troubadour (265 Old Brompton Road, SW5) stylishly bohemian, with poetry nights, live music, etc., a great spot to spend a night, and you can eat well here. Bar Italia (22 Firth Street, W1), is still worth the cost for its excellent coffee – there's nowhere quite like it in town for watching life pass by. Staying in Soho, Maison Bertaux (28 Greek Street, W1) was established 1871 and is still going strong – a real institution. Paul (29-30 Bedford Street, WC2) brings a little Gallic flair to London. Go west to Lisboa Patisserie (57 Goldborne Road, W10) close to the north end of Portobello market – a perfect place. On the other side of town, head to the Brick Lane Bagel Bakery (159 Brick Lane, E1; open 24 hours a day) for the best bagel in London.

Street markets

There are lots all over London, some for clothes, some for fruit and vegetables, and some old traditional meat or fish markets. The following are worth a diversion.

Smithfield, EC1 is London's meat market, the last of the big markets to survive in its original home. Smithfield (smooth field) has been associated with livestock for 900 years; it was originally a place to buy horses. Billingsgate Fish Market (Trafalgar Way, E14) is open to the public, but set the alarm clock; it's all over by 8am, and at its best around 6am. Other good food markets (fruit and veg) include tiny Berwick Street, W1 – well worth a visit – and Borough (Borough High Street, SE1: Fri/Sat only), for all things edible; a foodie's heaven. Similarly gourmet in style is the Farmers Market (Cramer Street car park, Marylebone High Street, W1, behind Waitrose; Sundays, 10am-2pm). For flowers, try the much-loved Columbia Road market (Bethnal Green, E2; Sundays, 8am-1pm); if you don't want to buy, go for the spectacle. Bermondsey (Long Lane, SE1, Fridays 4am-2pm) is London's biggest market for antiques and fine arts – a treat for early risers; bring a torch.

London's three most popular markets are its three biggest, selling anything and everything. Best known is Portobello Road, W11, which is open all week in some form, but it buzzes most on Friday and Saturday: cool

clothes, a pound of oranges, a Louis XV chair. Camden Market (Camden Town, NW1: daily, from 10am, best at weekends), is huge, comprises five markets in all, a top tourist destination for the young; if you want that pair of 1952-Levi XXs – or a piece of cyber-punk jewellery – the Stables Market, fun and adventurous, is the place to come. And the hot food stalls, from Chinese to Caribbean, are brilliant. Finally, Brick Lane, E1 (Sundays, 8am-1pm) is one of the few

magnets that manages to attract lazy North, South or West Londoners over to the East End. It is fantastic, a great scene, London's most interesting market (even if you don't buy a thing), a perfect Sunday morning experience. While you're here, explore the area's burgeoning funky design shops – and stop for one of its legendary curries. This is *the* place to eat Indian food in London.

Parks, heaths, gardens, fields and cemeteries

The cleverest of Londoners fall ill only in summer, and only when the sun's out. You will often find them sprawled out in their nearest park bravely recovering. There are hundreds of small parks, gardens and cemeteries all over London. You are more likely to chance upon them if you walk, or cycle, around. Ask your hosts and they should be able to point you in the direction of the local secret. The following are the bigger places you might like to visit, ill or not.

Central

Hyde Park, bang in the middle of town, for bike-riding, kite-flying, horse-riding, deck-chair-sleeping, people-watching, pleasure-boating, picnicking, on-line skating, even swimming in the Serpentine Lake. Check out the spectacular Italian water gardens at the Lancaster Gate entrance. Kensington Gardens forms the western side of the park and is where you'll find the Princess Diana Memorial Garden. You can walk all the way from Notting Hill to Parliament Square (about three miles) through Kensington Gardens, Hyde Park, Green Park and the most beautiful of London's central parks, St James's Park. The Serpentine Gallery in Kensington Gardens is open all year round, 10am-6pm, and admission is free. Speakers' Corner (Cumberland Gate, Marble Arch, W1; Sunday mornings) is a must for those in search of an argument; just bring your soapbox and you are free to say whatever you want. Alternatively, come to listen (and laugh).

North

Head to the Outer Circle in Regent's Park for London Zoo or the delightful Inner Circle for a hint of what Victorian pleasure gardens must have been like – a very special spot. Hampstead Heath is as wild as London gets. Parliament Fields gives views all over London. There are ponds to bathe in, you can even fish. Bands play in summer on Sunday afternoons. You'll forget you're anywhere near a city, let alone in the middle of one. A perfect place, as good in bad weather as in good. Primrose Hill is less touristy than its southern neighbour, Regent's Park, and more popular with locals for its views over London. Highgate Cemetery (Swain's Lane, N6), where Karl Marx is buried, is another glorious place, one not to be missed.

South east

Greenwich is a great day out, not least for its park that has at the summit of its hill the Royal Observatory gazing up to heaven. Henry VIII was born at Greenwich Palace and even though he took Hampton Court off Cardinal Wolsey's hands, Greenwich Palace remained his favourite residence; his daughters, Queens Mary and Elizabeth, were born here. It is London's biggest park, and you can avoid the traffic or tube by arriving by boat. Ferries run from Westminster Pier to Greenwich Pier every 40 minutes, all year round (first ferry 10.40am, last 3.20pm). It costs £6.50 one way, £8.20 return. If you have a travel card, you receive a one-third discount. The journey takes about one hour.

South west

Clapham Common hosts major events during the summer. It is not London's most beautiful green space – in winter it's positively bleak – but it gives Clapham a horizon; few districts in London have one of those. Down the hill form Clapham is the nicely old-fashioned Battersea Park, with bandstand, children's zoo, a pagoda by the Thames, rose gardens, boating pond – very popular with families on sunny Sunday afternoons. Further west is Barnes Common, another London gem, wild, and wildly beautiful. On weekends you may come across a cricket match as there are a couple of pitches where fattening forty year-olds still act out the odd dream. A couple of miles south west from Barnes and you find Richmond Park. If you visit only one park while in London, pick Richmond. It is London's biggest (though technically Richmond is not in London) and is more like being in the middle of the country. Wild woods, an eight-mile walking, running and cycling perimeter track, ponds, plantations and woods, a golf course, the wonderfully named Spankers Hill, and deer, of which there are many. An idyllic place. A little to the north of Richmond is Kew Gardens (the Royal Botanic Gardens at Kew, to give it its proper name: opens 9.30am, closes 4.30pm in winter, 6.30pm in summer, 020 8332 5655; admission £8.50) – 300 acres of tremendous beauty. It is a World Heritage site and worth coming simply to see and enter the huge Victorian greenhouses – absolute masterpieces. Kew has one of everything, be it tree, plant or shrub. There are many different gardens (bamboo, rose, azalea, palm, etc). It has the largest botanical collection in the world. You can arrive by boat from Westminster Pier (April-September); the journey takes about one and a half hours.

The Thames and the north-south divide

The Thames plays a strange role in present-day London life. It is not a river that binds a city, like the Seine in Paris or the Danube in Budapest. Its inhabitants do not criss-cross it ten times a day. In fact, the poor devils who live to its north hardly ever see it, and they venture across it only in times of pestilence and war. It is worth noting that North Londoners and South Londoners have wildly differing notions of their city and of its boundaries. Oddly enough, many North Londoners believe themselves to be South Londoners. They live in places like Chelsea or Victoria, or even Westminster, and have an 'S' for 'south' in their post code. This confuses them, for they live north of the river. Now, whatever disinformation you hear while in London, herein lies the truth: South London starts south of the river. It must follow, therefore, that North London starts north of the river – in SW3, W6, EC4, wherever. The divide in London has always been 'north' against 'south', with tribes from each land being noticeably different from each other. South Londoners are better-travelled than their northern counterparts, more open and gregarious, generally more worldly. A scientific study once proved conclusively that South Londoners are substantially more

intelligent than their backward cousins from the North. For their part, North Londoners see South Londoners as second-class citizens, peripheral figures, good-for-nothings, hardly Londoners at all. In return, South Londoners pity North Londoners and usually send them in the direction of France when they find them lost in Vauxhall, begging for directions. North Londoners experience great trauma south of the river and avoid it at all costs. It is for this reason that North Londoners expect their South London friends to meet them north of the river. South Londoners oblige; they would never see their friends if they did not. But when, in turn, they invite those friends south, they are met by nervous laughter,

lame excuses, or blatant lies. This is London, a tale of two cities.

As for the Thames, it just flows by mellifluously, ignoring the warring tribes, keeping the peace between them. It likes a little bit of green upon its banks, at least a path where Londoners can escape the roar of the city. Recently, the greed of property developers and local councils has seen its foreshore sold increasingly into bondage, a heinous act of betrayal for which those responsible should swing; at Westminster Bridge, where the Thames swirls, signalling its displeasure. But despite the unwelcome over-development of Thames-frontage and the ever-dwindling length of its riverside path, and despite the fact that few Londoners profess much affection for their river, the Thames cuts through London with sublime indifference, revealing its beauty only to those who look kindly upon it, while remaining a haze of muddy brown to those who don't. People who come to London and do not make a connection with it miss a beat of London's heart.

The most popular riverside walk these days is on the south side between Westminster Bridge and Bankside; concrete all the way, but very pretty and with plenty of diversions: the London Eye (the huge Ferris wheel), the bookstalls under

Waterloo Bridge, the South Bank, Gabriel's Wharf for restaurants, the Oxo Tower for its view of the City, and finally along to Tate Modern. Here, the Millennium Footbridge – the 'swaying' bridge that had to be closed, an act met with hoots of derisive laughter by Londoners – will take you across and directly up to St Paul's; a great Sunday stroll. Elsewhere, the Putney-Bridge/Hammersmith-Bridge loop is lovely, very wild on the south side (halfway along you can take a detour and visit the remarkable Wetlands Centre). You can stick to the south side at Hammersmith Bridge and head on up to Barnes, then cross the railway bridge and come back down to Hammersmith, or keep going to Mortlake, Chiswick, Kew, Richmond. You can walk all the way, or ride bikes. It's about eight miles to Richmond, and the south side really is prettier than the north, with pubs for sustenance on the way. Ducks and swans, oarsmen and fishermen, peace and quiet; don't miss it.

London books and literature

Peter Ackroyd's *London: the Biography* is exquisite: 2000 years of vibrant, stinking, wicked London – a tour de force. A N Wilson has followed suit (there's nothing like an original idea), and his version has also been well-received. *The London Encyclopaedia*, edited by Ben Weinreb and Christopher Hibbert, is a wonderful reference book, full of stories; no London home should be without one. The diaries of John Evelyn and Samuel Pepys evoke and illuminate 17th-century London; Boswell's *London Journal* (1762-1763), edited by Frederick A Pottle, does the same for 18th-century London. In literature, there tends to be a communal assumption that Dickens secured the patent rights for describing London, and it is perhaps for this reason that other writers have either steered clear of 'London as

character', or simply not been noticed for it. Those that have successfully brought London to life include Trollope, Wodehouse and

Graham Greene (*The End of the Affair*, *Ministry of Fear*), but the writer who owns London these days is Iain Sinclair; if you want to read contemporary fiction with London as more than a back drop, he's your man. Last, but not least, there's Gerald Kersh, who remains inexplicably undiscovered. His 1957 novel *Fowlers End* is to London what John Fante's *Ask the Dust* is to LA, or John Kennedy *Toole's Confederacy of Dunces* is to New Orleans. London rings from every page: mad, bad, and defiantly funny; a big comic novel.

Shopping

London's shops are among the best in the world. There are more tantalizing little boutiques than there ever were in the Sixties, heaps of delectable delicatessens, and more beautiful-than-ever flagship stores. This retail-utopia promises most to those with astronomical budgets, but there are pleasures in store for the browser too - whether roaming the cavernous acres of the 'top people's store' or dipping into the dusty delights on an antiquarian booksellers on the Charing Cross Road. And then there are the famous sales: January's (starting 26 December) and July's (usually, beginning June).

Oxford Street to Marylebone

London's most famous, and grid-locked, shopping street, a tidal wave of shopping-mad tourists, has one saving grace: Selfridges. Its ten fabulous acres house the largest range of lipsticks in Europe, the most exhilarating displays of food and fashion, the most magical windows at Christmas and, lately, the most exciting ranges of menswear. Once again, Selfridges is all things to all people. Escape the hoards of Oxford Street into the pedestrianised refuge of St Christopher's Place (essential pit stop: Carluccio's Caffe and shop), then on up to the charmingly old-fashioned Marylebone High Street, unlikely home to the chic and the off-beat. Visit Sixty 6 for funky 50s and 60s oddities; the Conran Shop, temple to homeware design; Daunt Books, serenely Edwardian, specialist in travel; V V Rouleaux, exquisite repository of tassels and trims; and modish Mint, Wigmore Street, for *objets*, textiles and glass.

Bloomsbury

Eastwards to the leafy and literary squares of Bloomsbury. For the best of modernist furniture (30s to 70s) head for the Target Gallery in Windmill Street; for an enticing selection of contemporary textiles, ceramics and glass, Contemporary Applied Arts in Percy Street. Drop into the British Museum Shop for a repro Celtic necklace, to Museum Street for outdoor cafés and shops brimming with curios and antiques,

then to New Oxford Street for James Smith & Son, eccentric purveyors of umbrellas. Or cut across to little Lambs Conduit Street for Persephone Books and their exquisite reprints of forgotten women's classics.

Clerkenwell

And on, ever eastwards, to oh-so-cool Clerkenwell. The French Huguenots established the area as a centre for clock-making and jewellery and now it is reinventing itself - a hotbed of architects and designers. Off the main drag of the Clerkenwell Road is Georgian Clerkenwell Green; don't miss the Lesley Craze Gallery, showcase for modern jewellers, and C2+ for one-off scarves and throws. Mini-parade Exmouth Market is home to elegant jewellery gallery, EC One, Space (classy kitsch), Inflate (blow-uppable everything), and Edible, London's top spot for chocolate-dipped scorpions and smoked cobra. You can eat here too (though you may prefer celebrated Moro, at No 34).

Bond Street to Piccadilly

Cut south from Oxford Street into New Bond Street and Old Bond Street (for absolute fabulousness, hard to beat) and slip into Savile Row for timeless tailoring - Gieves & Hawkes or outré Richard James. Thence to classy Burlington Arcade - taking great care not to carry large packages, hurry, whistle or hum (long banned) along your way – and make a bee-line for Picketts' delectable leather goods and scarves. And on to Piccadilly for Fortnum & Mason, founded in 1707, London's most stately store. The gilded eau-de-nil frontage hints at the grandeur within, the Food Hall is epicurean heaven, and for extravagant ice cream, the Fountain Restaurant is unmissable. At No 187 is Hatchards, booksellers by appointment to Her Majesty the Queen, elegant, olde-world and charming, and beyond, Jermyn Street, discreetly famous for shirts since 1700.

Regent Street

Up the grand sweep of Regent Street to London's most alluring store, Liberty, cherished as much for its 19th-century Arts and Crafts interior (even the lifts are oak-panelled) as for its distinctive 21st-century wares; the oriental rug bazaar is a joy. Tucked away behind Liberty is old Sixties hang-out Carnaby Street – a genteel shadow of its former cool self, but still geared towards youth fashion.

Soho

Traversing the garishness of Leicester Square, enter Soho, whose maze of streets teem with gay bars, late bars, Chinese food emporia and Berwick Street Market (fruit and veg). Fascinating Old Compton Street is home to the Algerian Coffee Stores,

founded in 1887, and I Camisa &
Son, crammed with olives, oils and
wild boar ham. Soho borders the
Charing Cross Road, famous for its
bookshops – rambling giant Foyles,
and 'lifestyle' bookstore Borders,
with coffee shop and comfy chairs.
If commercial booksellers are not
your thing, pop into Any Amount
of Books at No 62, a ramshackle
antiquarian/second-hand booksellers
with masses of charm, and
Zwemmers for its wonderful
photographic department (the rest
of this independent booksellers has
closed).

Covent Garden

It's a short stroll from here to
Covent Garden. Once London's
leading wholesale fruit, veg and
flower market, Covent Garden is a
tourist mecca that bounces with
shops and boutiques, open-air cafes
and pavement performers (London's
best). Away from the Market Hall
and Piazza is a cluster of small
streets teeming with quirky shops.
Head for Neal's Yard for holistic
treatments and vegan bakes, Neal
Street for Mango's Spanish fashion,
and cobbled Floral Street for Paul
Smith's playful take on (mostly)
men's fashion, and The Sanctuary,
London's most famous women's spa.

Notting Hill

Luxurious, bohemian Notting Hill.
Away from the Saturday throb of

Portobello (see Markets) are streets
lined with shops and boutiques for
an adventurous crowd. For kooky,
handmade hats head for Christine
Bec, Westbourne Park Road, and for
sumptuous designer furniture,
Carden Cunietti; to Ledbury Road for
Anya Hindmarch's witty handbags
and shoes, Simon Finch's rare books,
and Aimé's minimalist French
lifestyle goodies. For modern art in a
friendly setting try the East West
Gallery, and for cookbooks with their
own test kitchen, Books for Cooks -
both in Blenheim Crescent. In
Needham Road find Flow (cutting
edge crafts) and Miller Harris
(custom-made fragrances). And don't
miss Westbourne Grove: Traid, the
hippest charity chain in the UK, is
at No 61 (designer and vintage wear

at rock-bottom prices) and, at the western, covetable end, Christopher Farr's inspirational rugs, Emma Hope's beaded shoes and Tom (Conran)'s divine deli.

Kensington

If high street stores are what you're after (Muji, Gap, Zara) Kensington High Street provides a gentle alternative to Oxford Street - while groovy lifestyle shop Urban Outfitters has its finger on the youth pulse. Kensington Church Street is worth diving into for antiques and rare treats.

Holland Park

Neighbouring Holland Park is home to the chicest cul-de-sac in London, Clarendon Cross. French, whimsical kitchenware (old and new) from Summerill & Bishop, antique clothes from Virginia, retro florals (peg-bags and pyjamas) from Cath Kidston, and the *dernier cri* in exquisite things – from camisoles to candles – at The Cross.

Chelsea

The King's Road is as dashing a thoroughfare as it was in its Sixties heyday. Head for Heal's (at 234) or Designer's Guild (267) for characterful home furnishings; the Sundance Market (250) for all things organic; Rococo (321) for exceptional chocolates; Brora (344) for classic-contemporary knits;

Couverture (310) for cocooning, quirky bedlinen; Steinberg & Tolkein (193) for vintage couture. And in the Fulham Road is Conran's flagship store.

Knightsbridge

If designer names are your passion, Sloane Street is your strip. From modish Prada and uber-chic Marni to vivid Versace, this Knightsbridge avenue reeks of class. Queening it at the top end is Harvey Nichols, style shrine for ladies who lunch. And then there's Harrods (before you sweep in, make a quick detour to charming Pont Street and dazzling Beauchamp Place). Al Fayed's fiefdom is virtually a self-contained empire, the lumbering maiden aunt to Harvey Nicks' soigné cousin, but it is the bastion of British retailing, and worth a visit if only for the magnificent toy department, all on one floor. (Hamleys' more famous toys are spread over many.) On a final, practical note – make sure you leave your rucksack and ripped jeans behind; if not, the doormen in the green top hats may send you packing.

Shopping section
Jo Boissevain